SUCCESS WITH HEART FAILURE

Help and Hope for Those with Congestive Heart Failure

SUCCESS WITH HEART FAILURE

Help and Hope for Those with Congestive Heart Failure

Marc A. Silver, M. D.

Foreword by
Jay N. Cohn, M. D.

 INSIGHT BOOKS

PLENUM PRESS • NEW YORK AND LONDON

Library of Congress Cataloging-in-Publication Data

Silver, Marc A.
    Success with heart failure : help and hope for those with
congestive heart failure / Marc A. Silver.
        p.   cm.
    Includes bibliographical references and index.
    ISBN 0-306-44767-3
    1. Congestive heart failure--Popular works.   I. Title.
    [DNLM: 1. Heart Failure, Congestive--therapy.   WG 370 S587s 1994]
RC685.C53S56   1994
616.1'29--dc20
DNLM/DLC
for Library of Congress   94-28255
                                                               CIP

Although this book provides dosage and other information on specific medications and treatments, this information should not in any way be considered or used as direct prescriptive advice for any child or adult. You should consult your personal physician before beginning any medical treatment.

ISBN 0-306-44767-3

© 1994 Marc A. Silver
Insight Books is a Division of Plenum Publishing Corporation
233 Spring Street, New York, N.Y. 10013-1578

An Insight Book

Printed in the United States of America

To all my patients—the brave men and women who have taught me, through their suffering, wisdom and intelligence, how better to help them

Foreword

We are going through a highly appropriate revolution in our society. People want and are being encouraged to play a more active role in the decision-making processes that may affect their lives. Nowhere is this more obvious than in medicine, where the omnipotent physician should no longer be aloof from the questions of his or her patients. Diagnostic and treatment strategies are increasingly being shared with patients and their families.

Heart failure is a disease that afflicts so many Americans and has such an impact on the individual and his or her family, friends, and associates that its diagnosis and management is the business of many people besides the doctor. In order to understand the disease well enough to appreciate the lifestyle alterations and medical treatments imposed, a book aimed at all who are involved in this problem is most timely.

Marc Silver has had a longstanding interest in the management of the patient with heart failure. He brings his considerable experience to this new book aimed at providing the lay as well as professional reader with insights about the disease and its treatment. Some of the sophistications about treatment strategies haven't yet penetrated into all doctors' offices, so health care workers as well as patients may have much to learn about this condition.

As a new health care system evolves in the United States, it is likely that more and more responsibility will fall on the patient to ferret out the best medical care. Disincentives for health care workers to utilize expensive technology and to refer to subspecialists will place an increased burden on the patient to participate in his or her own health care. Understanding one's own disease is a prerequisite for making the choices and demands that may be effective in improving outcomes.

This book should be a useful supplement to office and hospital visits for afflicted individuals. Since a well-informed patient is likely to get better medical care than an indifferent one, the product of this book should be better quality and duration of life for the millions who suffer from heart failure.

Jay N. Cohn, M.D.
Professor of Medicine
Head, Cardiovascular Division
University of Minnesota Medical School
Minneapolis, Minnesota

Acknowledgments

If after reading this book you do not find it useful or helpful for yourself or for a friend or relative, consider the book, in its entirety, my doing. On the other hand, if you gain some knowledge, some insight, or some hope for yourself or a loved one, recognize that the people mentioned in the following paragraphs are some of those who made it happen.

My deepest gratitude goes to my beloved parents, my late father, Sam, and my dear mother, Ida, who brought me into this world to do something good—I hope I have, at least in part, fulfilled their dreams—and to my "younger" sister, Betty Ann, and her family, who have been a support forever. I appreciate all the help Betty Ann gave me along the way; she will never know why I think she is the strong one.

My patients have been a constant source of knowledge and support. In sharing their hearts and emotions with me, they have given me a great gift. One in particular, Joan Hemzacek, asked me to teach her about heart failure and made me become a better doctor. In many ways she is responsible for this book.

On a daily basis I am grateful for the work I do and even more grateful that I have had dedicated nursing professionals working with me over the years with the expertise and vision to better the lives of those who have heart failure. They include Carol Keeler, Diana Merz, Anne Tucker, Jean Hughes, Lorraine Heany, Patti Dahl, Beth Mangal-Ian, Caroline Blakley, Cyndi Koeppen, Bea Wolfe, Nancy Schwabauer, Julie Kozlowski, and Joanne Cuny. I am equally grateful for the many exercise physiologists who have been so helpful, particularly Jess Toussaint and Kathy Lennon. Thanks also to Jeannine Pfau, R.D., who helped me with sections in this book on dietary restrictions and sodium content of foods.

I also thank my mentors, including Dr. William C. Roberts, Dr. Joseph Messer, and Dr. Karl T. Weber, who showed me in words and deeds what hard work is all about. And to all my former and present colleagues at the National Heart, Lung and Blood Institute; Rush Presbyterian St. Lukes Medical Center; Loyola University; the University of Chicago; the University of Illinois; Michael Reese Hospital; and Midwest Heart Specialists I extend my gratitude.

I want to thank Dr. Fred Weinstein, who single-handedly did so much to help me become a physician—I don't know if I have ever thanked him enough. Dr. Robert Kark took a young intern aside for breakfast one morning and put a career on course; he too has probably not been thanked adequately. I am certainly grateful to and appreciate the trust of the many physicians, both locally and from around the country, who send me patients for evaluation.

This book had many passages. It sat in my head for about 4 years. The next passage came when my dear friends Allan and Gail Muehrcke got tired of hearing about "the book" and banished me for 2 days to their summer cottage, where the initial chapters took form. I thank Julie R. Dunne and Bruce Wexler, who helped guide this book to the next passage, putting it on the proper path toward publication. I thank Frank Darmstadt and Jennifer Reynolds of Insight Books, who had insight into the idea that heart failure is something people need to read about. Also, thanks to Trudy Brown for production assistance, and to Toby Troffkin for superb copyediting. I thank Maureen "Moe" Pipal, who typed the manuscript beautifully even under the occasional pressure of deadlines gone by. And to Joanne Colandrea, my administrative assistant, who points me in the right direction on a daily basis, I say thank you.

I thank those friends and colleagues who critically read parts or all of the book, including Dr. Jay Cohn; Dr. Spencer Kubo; Dr. Thomas Rector; Dr. Ileana Pina; Dr. Mahboubeh Eghbali; Dr. Michael Rich; Dr. Stuart Rich; Dr. Margaret Redfield; Dr. Barry Uretsky; Carol Keller, R.N., M.S.; Sue Nelson, L.P.N.; Ms. Julie Procich; Mr. James Duncan; and Ms. Anne Berger.

Finally, for my wife, Laureen, and my children— Zachary, Adam, Nora, Ryan, Jacob, and Meredith—I am eternally grateful. They know that helping patients is a sacred duty for me and have yielded their time with me when I know it was difficult. It is said that one must choose a mate wisely, for that single choice will determine more than 90% of one's happiness in life. I chose wisely and from that decision has sprung forth all else good in my life. (Little does my family know of my plans to write another book!!)

To everyone who has touched my path, I give thanks.

How to Read This Book

This book is organized into sections: discussing what heart failure is, how one gets it, how it's diagnosed, how it's treated, and so forth. I have tried to make the flow as natural and logical as possible. I have also tried to make this book readable for everyone who picks it up. Therefore, I have made an attempt to explain some of the complex concepts regarding heart failure and cardiac physiology and pathology in terms that everyone will understand. On the other hand, I've tried not to make it so simple that other health care professionals will dismiss it and not find anything useful in it.

The reader may find some redundancy, since several of the key concepts in treating heart failure recur throughout the book. Finally, I have included several appendixes at the end of the book that provide more detail, including photographs of hearts, and list references I think the reader will find useful.

I think most readers will find it useful before plunging into the main chapters to read the Introduction and the Foreword and to then take a moment and look through Appendix I, which is a glossary of heart failure terms. This should help familiarize you with some of the terms that are used in the text and may provide a basis for understanding as you begin to read the text. As you read through the text, you may want to stop and consult the appendixes to look up a term, to check a drug, or to look at some of the photographs I have included.

I hope you will use this book as I have intended it—as a resource that you can return to time and again to enhance your understanding of heart failure.

Contents

Introduction

I have written this book because my entire professional career has been dedicated to taking care of patients with heart failure. Needing to learn about their disease, my patients have for the most part acquired the information bit by bit from me and my skilled and dedicated staff of heart failure nurses. However, the time has come to put all the information into a single source book to help many more patients and their families.

I have also written this book because over the years I have been impressed with how little many patients know about heart failure when they first come to see me, how scared or angry they are, and how transformed they are when they gain some insight into their disease and take some responsibility for their health. Richard Bloch, cofounder of H&R Bloch, Inc., wrote an inspiring book for cancer patients, called *Fighting Cancer*, in which he gives information and inspiration but emphasizes that the patient's initial step is a commitment to understand and battle the cancer. The goal of this book is not only to give information but to motivate patients and their families to learn more about heart failure so that they can participate in their care—in current language, become "proactive."

I don't think I know a physician nowadays who does not subscribe to the belief that an informed patient is a better patient. However, a gap sometimes exists between the large amount of information patients hear and what they perceive, filter, understand, and retain. This book, hopefully, will give patients the opportunity to review many of the bits of information they have already been told and to blend them together into an understanding that fits their own individual situation.

Heart failure is a major national health care problem. Not a day goes by that we don't hear about some well-known figure who has died of heart failure. This year almost 500,000 persons will die of heart failure and over a million will be hospitalized by this disease process; by contrast, less than 50,000 will succumb to AIDS. Why, then, has there been so little written on such an important topic? My first guess would be because heart failure is not "sexy" enough: it predominantly affects the elderly, it is a chronic disease, and there is nothing new about it. Nothing new except that now it is a major health care problem. On the other hand, there has been a great deal of ongoing, intense interest in heart failure at the professional level. Unfortunately, information about much of this progress has filtered slowly to the general public. In this book I try to generate more interest in heart failure by the general public and to inform them of the advances being made in understanding and treating it.

Success with Heart Failure is the result of my desire to combine the lessons I have learned from my patients and some of the things my staff and I teach them into a readable text so that other patients, family members, physicians, nurses, technicians, hospital administrators—

actually anyone who is involved with heart failure—may learn and be stimulated to fight the disease. It is intended to serve as a primer on heart failure and a resource that patients can refer to time and again.

As a physician, it is easy for me to lose sight of the fact that medicine has very few absolute truths. I want to make clear that the opinions contained within this book are mine—and mine in a contemporary framework. Changes evolve in medicine today more rapidly than ever before. This book is not written with the intent to diagnose or treat a particular individual. Since no two individuals are identical, this book is intended as a general resource and guide. My best advice to you is to always consult your own physician and together with him or her seek what is best for you and your loved one. All tests, treatments, and especially medications and dosages should be reviewed with your physician; neither the author nor the publisher assumes responsibility for omissions or errors. Often, after I talk to a new patient but even before I examine him or her, I am asked, "Well, Doc, what do you think?" I realize how anxious patients are and also how impatient some readers may be to acquire information about heart failure and ensure that they or a loved one receive the best possible care. Remember that the process may be a tedious one. Take your time in reading the chapters, reread what you don't understand, and then begin a dialogue with the doctor involved.

I invite each of you to write to me and share your thoughts on how else this book could be of benefit to you. I also invite physicians to contact me with their opinions or comments. It is really every member of the team—patient, family members, allied health personnel, and physicians— who is involved in the treatment of heart failure.

Finally, although I have already acknowledged them

at the beginning of this book, I want to once again thank the many patients I have treated over the years. These brave men, women, and, occasionally, children have so inspired me and sustained me! They have tolerated my endless questioning on various aspects of their lives— their emotions, attitudes, and lifestyle. Among other things, they have brought in their medical and drug bills, permitted me to talk with their spouses and families open- ly, and, most of all, become my friends. For their sake, I hope that major advances will soon be made in the treat- ment and prevention of heart diseases that eventuate in heart failure and that this book is soon outdated. In other words, I wish them success with heart failure!

Chapter 1

Don't Be Angry

Many years ago when I began writing this book, this was the first chapter I wrote. I discarded it early on but later decided to include it. I feel I must say a few words about anger and emotions before we delve into other topics. Heart failure, in reality, is commonly a chronic disease process, meaning that while there is often not a complete cure, there are ways to improve and stabilize the condition and certainly better ways to understand and live with it. However, when most patients initially hear the words "heart failure," which is indeed an unfortunate term, they equate this with fatality, and an array of emotions emerges —or, more often, *don't* emerge—and eventually impacts on relationships the patient has with physicians, nurses, and family members.

We know from the important work done by Dr. Elizabeth Kübler-Ross (*On Death and Dying*) and others that when patients are told they have a terminal illness, a form of cancer, for example, they pass through several emotional stages until they reach a level of acceptance. Even when patients are told they have systemic hypertension, or high blood pressure (which can be very well controlled and treated but usually requires lifelong dietary and medical therapy), a similar reaction occurs. Therefore, it is not un-expected that anger ensues when patients hear they have heart failure. Part of the problem is a lack of understand-ing of what heart failure is and what can be done for it (hence, this book). However, even an insightful under-standing of heart failure leads to the notion that life some-how will be different, will include more medical care, and will inevitably be shortened. Who wouldn't be angry or upset? My advice, then, really is *do* be angry—but only for a period sufficient to work through those emotions and get more information and help. Then, don't be angry!

In general, anger is not a useful emotion unless it motivates the individual to do more to improve the situa-tion. Once the individual acts on this motivation, the knowledge and acceptance that result should eventually melt away the anger. If, instead, the anger remains, the use of any knowledge or understanding will be inhibited by this powerful emotion.

In caring for patients awaiting heart transplantation, I have observed that in those who wait prolonged periods of time for a donor to become available (and the wait may extend for months or years!) the predominant emotion is anger—anger over the wait, the chronicity of their illness, and their fate in having heart disease. Moreover, they re-main angry when their long-awaited goal comes to frui-tion, and the anger persists into the posttransplant period, preventing them from fully appreciating the gift they have received. These patients alienate family and friends and lose support systems they desperately need.

I have no magic formula by means of which patients can learn how to work through the initial anger and let it melt away into a better understanding. In some cases, anger over an illness simply serves to underscore a lifelong hostility or poor interpersonal relationships. In my experience, however, in most cases the following factors serve to allow patients to pass through the stage of anger:

1. A complete understanding of heart failure, including its causes, the nature of the testing required, and the treatments available
2. Good communication with their physician, with the nursing staff, and with their support systems, that is, family, friends, or even other patients with heart failure
3. Improvement in how they feel (even minor changes in treatment can cause significant improvement in how patients feel, and even slight improvement can alter how they feel about their disease and how willing they are to accept further information and treatment)
4. A feeling of empowerment, that is, of being in control of and responsible for the decisions in their care

Actually, all four factors are interrelated but may characterize distinct stages.

It is critical for patients to experience some improvement in how they feel. Even when a cardiologist asks me to see a patient for consideration for experimental heart failure treatment, I always carefully review all aspects of the patient's current therapy to see what modifications, albeit minor, can be performed with conventional therapies so that he or she can "feel better." This almost always restores hope to patients and their family and serves to motivate them to let go of their anger, thus enabling them to become more accepting and understanding of their illness and more motivated to participate in their future care. Feelings of empowerment are also important. I am reminded of a patient who shared her thoughts with me when I told her that she was in control of the decision regarding heart transplantation as a treatment for her advanced form of heart failure. She reminded me that the gift availability of the donor heart was not her decision, that she had no control over the computer matchup of her need and the potential donor heart, and that some of the medical decisions would depend on her physicians' evaluation of her condition, which was again not in her control. However, she concluded that the bottom-line decisions were hers. She recognized that they were shared decisions but that most of life's decisions can be characterized in just this way. Thinking things through in this fashion enabled this woman, who was an interesting person and, I think, the very first patient who sat in my office for hours reading my cardiology textbooks, to maintain a feeling of empowerment. It was her struggle to take control and learn about her disease and options that started me on a different path, a path not just of delivering medical care but of being a teacher, which is what the Latin word *doctor* means.

Let me emphasize as you read the chapters ahead that there are different positions along the anger–acceptance spectrum. A patient's reaction to information and suggestions depends on his or her position. Just as I expect my patients to react differently, so too do I expect each of you to have a different reaction. However, allow yourself to accept the information and perhaps review it many times. Not all of the information will fit your individual situation, but most of it will. I hope that your journey from anger to understanding and motivation will be brief and that you will be guided by the remainder of this book.

Chapter 2

The Challenge of Heart Failure

Are you one of the 3.5 million Americans living with heart failure? Or among the 1 million people who will be hospitalized with heart failure in the United States this year? Or one of the many millions more who are asymptomatic now but at high risk for developing heart failure in the near future? Will your spouse or parent be one of the nearly half-million new cases to be diagnosed this year? Are you a 65-year-old man whose heart failure was caused by years of untreated high blood pressure? Or a young woman whose diagnosis seemed to come out of the blue, with even your doctors unable to identify the cause? Have you been struck by the most common cause for hospitalization in people over the age of 65? Yet heart failure affects not only the elderly; it affects the young as well (the young rock star Jim Morrison died of heart failure).

If you answered yes to any of the preceding questions, I have good news: You obviously are not alone! The purpose of this book is to show you that there is hope, help, and treatment for all forms of heart failure. Despite what you might have heard—and even if you heard it from your doctor—heart failure is not an automatic death sentence. It is, however, one of the most misunderstood diseases around; people regularly confuse heart failure with heart attacks. The disease's literal name is certainly disheartening; failure connotes a frightening finality. But while you may not be able to beat heart failure, you can live with it. Over the years I have rarely seen a patient I couldn't help feel better or live longer. Heart failure patients I first met in their forties are living full, satisfying lives in their sixties. I've had senior citizens who looked as if they were at death's door make amazing progress with the right attitude and treatment.

In fact, those are the keys for everyone—attitude and treatment. With the right dosages of both, you can usually improve your condition dramatically. Unfortunately, we often encounter the wrong attitudes and/or the wrong treatments.

"You Have One Month to Live"

As I will discuss later, the amazing growth in our knowledge of coronary artery disease and heart attack is what has attracted much of the interest of researchers, patients, and physicians. And while most doctors know a great deal about coronary disease, they have shown relatively little interest in heart failure. Even today, many physicians incorrectly feel there have been almost no major advances in the diagnosis and treatment of heart failure—and this is true not only of general practitioners but of cardiologists as well!

Medicine has indeed made great strides in treating heart attack victims and people with clogged arteries, and

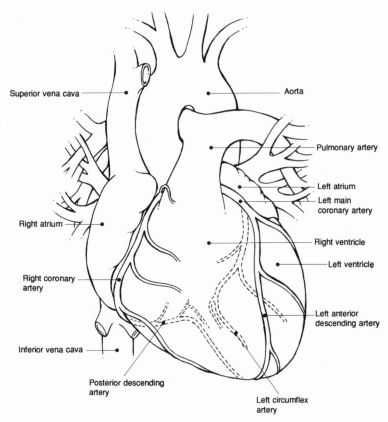

Superior vena cava

Aorta

Pulmonary artery

Left atrium

Left main coronary artery

Right atrium

Right ventricle

Left ventricle

Right coronary artery

Left anterior descending artery

Inferior vena cava

Posterior descending artery

Left circumflex artery

Figure 2.1. This figure depicts the external structure of the normal human heart. There are four chambers: the two upper chambers (right atrium and left atrium) and two lower chambers (right ventricle and left ventricle). Blood from the upper and lower parts of the body return to the heart via the superior vena cava and the inferior vena cava. Also shown are the major arteries which carry the blood from the right ventricle to the lung (pulmonary artery) and from the left ventricle to the head and the rest of the body (aorta). Immediately branching off the aorta are the coronary arteries, which supply blood directly to the heart muscle. The main coronary arteries are the left main, left anterior descending, left circumflex, and the right coronary artery. (Figure courtesy of Abbott Laboratories, Abbott Park, Illinois.)

doctors feel a great deal of satisfaction when they help bedridden patients become well again through angioplasty procedures, bypass operations, or other treatments. These treatments have also become relatively routine. In a nutshell, coronary disease is where the action is. Treating heart failure patients, on the other hand, has in the past not provided most doctors with the same sense of satisfaction. Surgical treatments for heart failure are the exception rather than the rule. Often, a heart failure patient lives with a great deal of uncertainty, requires frequent office visits, and experiences no major leaps of improvement from visit to visit. Slow progress is often funneled into depression or anger or frustration by the patient, the family, and even the physician. Treatment can be quite complicated, since heart failure may trigger other medical problems and result in additional complications (with the liver or kidneys, for example). Moreover, these additional problems cannot always be treated in the usual ways because of the limitations, interactions, and side-effect concerns imposed by the person's heart failure. Consequently, a percentage of doctors don't keep up with new developments in the heart failure field, preferring to focus instead on coronary disease. They labor under anachronistic notions about treatment, and some, unfortunately, inadvertently cause some patients to give up hope.

I can't tell you the number of people who have come to me and said, "My doctor told me I only have one month to live" or "My doctors say they've done all they can for me." I always tell my patients, "Doctors are not God; no one knows how long you have to live" or "I'm sure there's something I can do for you." I don't say this just to make them feel better (though it does) but because it's true. People sentenced to short-term survival often survive for many productive years! Some simply need simple medication adjustments. Others need better education and counseling on salt restriction. Someone who hasn't responded to traditional treatment may respond to an experimental procedure. Once patients simply realize that there are scores of things left to try and that there's a good chance at least one of them will work, their conditions often improve. This is due not only to the beneficial effect of a positive mental attitude but to the fact that patients become more active participants in their treatment. For example, they become acutely aware of changes in how they feel and report those changes to their doctors, who then vary treatments accordingly; they watch their diet and weight carefully, making sure they stay within the doctor's recommendations; and they take their medicine in the right amounts at the right times (heart failure patients often take a number of medications, and depressed or elderly patients frequently forget to take their pills or take them at the wrong times).

Of course, none of this matters if a doctor prescribes Pill A when the patient should be receiving Pill B. This happens not because the doctor is negligent but simply because he or she is following an older, more traditional, approach. For instance, digoxin is a common drug prescribed for heart failure patients that, among other things, can help the heart pump blood more strongly. This is fine for people who have a systolic problem (*systole* being the heart's contracting function, designed to squeeze blood out), but a diastolic problem (*diastole* being the relaxation of the heart between contractions) usually should *not* be treated with that drug. Digoxin causes a hard-pumping heart to pump even harder, which can have disastrous consequences, or at the very least involve the risk and expense of an additional potent heart medication.

This differentiation of heart failure into a particular

type is no trivial problem. Interestingly, in patients under the age of 65 the usual (about 70% of the time) predominant problem in heart failure is a systolic one, or a weak pumping action of the heart; that means, however, that fully 30% of these patients in fact have a relaxation or diastolic problem that is causing their heart failure. Moreover, as much as 70% of heart failure problems in the elderly is related to poor relaxation of the heart muscle, or diastolic dysfunction. As you will see later, the problem is that treatments for these different forms of heart failure are in fact quite different; certain forms of treatment for systolic failure (poor contraction of the heart muscle) may make a person with diastolic failure (poor relaxation of the heart muscle) much worse. Because the symptoms of systolic and diastolic heart failure are often the same, it's difficult to determine the cause through cursory testing. It's easy for doctors to mistakenly jump to a conclusion and head down the wrong treatment path.

What Is Heart Failure, Anyway?

The main purpose of this chapter is to first clear the air and define what heart failure is. As I said earlier, the term itself is ominous, but unfortunately it is one we are stuck with for now. I suspect that you are reading this book because either you, your spouse, your parent, or a close friend or relative has some form of heart failure, which is now commonly called *congestive heart failure* (CHF) but in the old days was referred to as dropsy. Recently I gave a talk to one of our local chapters of the Mended Hearts Organization, a support group for people who primarily have cardiovascular problems. I asked for a show of hands as to how many people in the audience knew of someone, whether a spouse, relative, or neighbor, who had heart failure. Nearly two-thirds of the audience raised their hand. I then asked for people to define what heart failure was. There were few accurate answers.

Now any second-year medical student can give you the traditional definition of heart failure, namely, the inability of the cardiac function to meet the metabolic needs of the body. Unfortunately, that does not explain what heart failure truly is. I think the best way for people to think of the heart is to picture it as a pump whose job is to pump blood, which carries oxygen, or the fuel our bodies use, to the rest of the body—including arms, legs, abdomen, liver, kidneys, and brain. Simply stated, then, heart failure is a condition in which the heart does not adequately perform its duties as a pump of blood. It is clear that a variety of malfunctions with the heart can potentially cause heart failure. We will discuss many of those in other chapters in this book. It is also obvious that if heart failure simply represents the failure of the heart to work as it should as a pump, then there may well be degrees of heart failure. And in fact this is true. Again, in other chapters in this book we will discuss how the kind of heart failure and its degree of severity are determined.

The main intent of this book is to demystify the very difficult and complex disease entity called heart failure and clarify for patients, family, and friends what heart failure is really all about. I want to talk not only about what heart failure is but about what can be done for it in both conventional and nonconventional ways. I will talk about who should be helping patients care for their heart failure and about what patients can do to help their doctor and health care professionals care for them. I'm truly hoping that each and every individual who reads this book will come away with a better understanding of what heart failure means today in the 1990s. I hope that that understanding will extend not only to patients and their families but to other individuals in the health care field, including hospital administrators, and even, God help us, to the politicians who are going to continue to have an impact on the priorities for health care in this country.

In fact, heart failure really is a national problem because of the striking demographics of this disease. As I mentioned earlier, there are well over 3.5 million people in the United States, or approximately 1% of our entire population, who have heart failure. And the number of cases keeps growing. The number of deaths related to heart failure alone has increased over fourfold in the last 20 years, a period in which we have waged a relatively successful war against death due to heart attack and stroke, achieving a significant decline in the mortality rate of both. In part, this increase in number of people with heart failure is related to our success in preventing patients from dying of heart attacks. As we all know, patients may survive several heart attacks and may undergo one or more bypass surgeries. Patients who survive their acute attacks may suffer damage to the heart muscle and eventually develop heart failure. The other common factor underlying the major increase in the number of heart failure cases each year is the aging of our population. As people age, they carry with them the cumulative subtle damages to the heart muscle brought on by coronary disease and high blood pressure; the longer one lives, the greater the likelihood of eventually developing some kind of pump problem. In fact, heart failure becomes increasingly common as people age, affecting about 10% of all people over the age of 75. The number one cause of hospitalization throughout this country for people over the age of 65 is heart failure. Between 1973 and 1986 the number of patients being discharged from a hospital with a diagnosis of heart failure more than doubled. While hospitalization rates remained fairly stable for patients between 35 and 54 years of age, there was a substantial increase in the number of elderly patients being hospitalized, with the most significant increase being in patients over the age of 74.

However, the increase in the prevalence of heart failure is not simply a problem related to aging. Even when the age factor is adjusted in statistical analysis, the death rate from heart failure continues to increase twofold, suggesting that other factors are operating here. Suffice it to say that heart failure is an extremely common medical problem that is increasing at an enormous rate both within the United States and throughout the world. It is a problem that is taxing our medical resources and affecting the daily lives of millions of men and women and their families and friends.

One of the slides I show to physicians when I talk about heart failure is labeled *Heart Failure: The Challenge for the Nineties*. I readily acknowledge that heart failure may not surpass in importance the issue of global peace or our federal deficit, but it ranks high in terms of a major medical epidemic. We need to face this challenge at all levels in order to convert our failures into successes.

Soon I'm going to talk about some of the common causes of heart failure, what you can do to possibly prevent it, and so forth, but I do want to spend a moment discussing the statistics, or what I call the good, the bad, and the ugly of heart failure. I think these relate to questions that are on everyone's mind, and I want to clear the air as well as set the stage for the information I am about to present in this book.

Now if one considers the statistics for even a decade ago for survival after developing heart failure, things look pretty dismal. The overall death rate from congestive heart failure within the first year of diagnosis was right around 50%. The good news is that today, with optimal medical treatment, that percentage has dropped below 10% for patients with good prognostic profiles, and it is quite reasonable to expect a 5-year survival rate of well beyond 50%. If you are reading this book and have a very mild form of heart failure, you may find these statistics quite sobering, and that is one of the reasons I prefer not to quote statistics to my patients initially. These statistics tend to lump together a great many patients with a variety of different risk factors and with different forms of heart failure. There are marked differences in the outcome of heart failure, and I want to mention some of the factors that account for them.

First of all, it is commonly asked whether one sex or the other seems to have a worse prognosis with heart failure. Some studies have suggested that men have a slightly worse prognosis (60% versus 45% for the 5-year mortality rate), but other studies have suggested that women have worse outcomes. I would say that, on balance, men and women seem to have the same risk of mortality. It is clear, however, that older patients do worse than younger patients, as was seen recently in a large study called the Studies of Left Ventricular Dysfunction (SOLVD), which suggested that younger patients with heart failure, aged 22 to 55, averaged a 17% one-year mortality rate whereas patients over the age of 76 had a 38% one-year mortality rate. Other risk factors, such as diabetes, atrial fibrillation (which is an irregular heartbeat of the upper chambers of the heart), and a history of smoking and alcohol consumption, also cause a worse prognosis. Interestingly, mortality in black patients seems to be about $1\frac{1}{2}$ times higher than in white patients overall, and the reasons for these differences in mortality are not clear.

The problem with statistics for heart failure is that they are just that. Statistics cannot predict what will happen to you or your friend or relative. In fact, no doctor can predict how long someone with heart failure will live. There are various tools that we use to help us guesstimate what might happen in the future, but let me assure you that no one has a crystal ball. In the chapters ahead I will review some of these tools, but, again, none of these are perfect. Nothing pleases me more than to see patients outlive their predicted survival statistics.

I think the lessons to be learned here are that there has been progress in the diagnosis and treatment of heart failure and that these advances have had significant impact on the overall prognosis. The flip side of the coin, however, is that with the growing prevalence of heart failure in our population we need to intensify our efforts at finding new and better ways to diagnose, treat, and ultimately prevent heart failure.

How Do You Get Heart Failure?

As soon as your doctor diagnoses you with heart failure, you should immediately ask the $64,000 question: What caused it? Your doctor may know from your past medical history, or he or she may do a series of tests to help determine the cause. If, however, you get a vague answer like "We always see this in older folks" or "A little bit of heart failure never hurt anybody," you may already be on the wrong path (see Chapter 4).

The odds are that you'll greatly enhance the effectiveness of your treatment if you pinpoint the cause. In fact, there are many forms of heart failure that are not only treatable but curable! The key, then, is to first determine the exact cause. The problem, of course, is that there are many causes (see Chapter 3 for a table listing the types of heart failure and their causes).

High blood pressure, or *hypertension*, is a major cause of heart failure, and there are over 60 million Americans who have it. If we could adequately treat those people, we could make a serious dent in the overall number of patients with heart failure in this country. It is estimated that even among those who know they have high blood pressure, not more than 25% are really treated adequately. In addressing this problem we must, I believe, put to rest two common myths. One is that high blood pressure means the blood pressure is *always* above normal. The truth is that high blood pressure does not mean a person has an elevated blood pressure all of the time. However, the blood pressure of those who have it goes above the normal limits on occasion; the more often this occurs and the greater the extent to which their blood pressure exceeds those limits, the greater the "load" of their high blood pressure and, often, the greater the risk of damage they might sustain to their heart, kidneys, eyes, or brain. The other myth we must abandon is the notion that our blood pressure should equal 100 plus our age. This is pure hogwash. In countries where salt is not a major ingredient in the diet and exercise is more common even among the elderly, this is simply not true. With our ever-increasing elderly population, we need to educate everyone about high blood pressure even more zealously now than ever before.

The abuse of alcohol or drugs can also cause heart failure. There is a general belief, promoted by the mass media, that alcohol is beneficial for the heart. (I remember clearly my beloved grandfather taking a shot of whiskey daily before meals until he died in his ninth decade of life.) However, while there is some evidence that limited alcohol may be helpful in preventing some forms of heart problems related to the coronary arteries, there is clear evidence that alcohol is a definite toxin, or damaging substance, to the heart muscle. Therefore, whether a person's heart failure was caused by years of alcohol abuse or not, I recommend that alcohol be avoided forever. I usually tell my patients that they may enjoy a single alcoholic beverage on Christmas, their wedding anniversary, or their birthday—but that's it. When they ask about once a month and then once a week, or even two or three times a week, I usually suspect that they may in fact have an alcohol problem. I forbid my patients to have alcohol at all and help those who cannot comply to seek counseling.

Other causes of heart failure include the following: blocked heart arteries, even with no history of a heart attack (coronary artery disease); heart attack, which may be a "silent" one the patient isn't aware of; inflammation of heart muscle, which may accompany a simple cold or flu-like illness and is often caused by a virus that settles in the heart muscle; narrowed or leaky heart valves, which can result from rheumatic fever, congenital problems, or even an aging process; numerous blood transfusions (the repeated transfusions required because of a genetic or acquired blood problem can create iron buildup in the heart); pregnancy (see Chapter 11); and AIDS, or acquired immunodeficiency syndrome (see Chapter 11).

Doctors may tell their patients that the cause of their heart failure is *idiopathic dilated cardiomyopathy*. What this scientific-sounding phrase really means is "We don't know what caused your heart muscle to weaken." This is an especially troublesome situation because doctors are unable to tie treatment to a specific cause. I will refer to these different causes of heart failure later, but let us now address a common question, namely, "How can I lessen my risk of developing heart failure?"

Prevention

Because of heart failure's many causes, preventative measures are so far only partially effective. Nevertheless, the following motto, which I recently shared with the audience at a lecture on geriatric heart failure, is useful: "The cure for heart failure in the elderly is prevention of cardiovascular disease in the young." Certainly you should do everything possible to lower high blood pressure and to follow the commonsense advice about not smoking, watching your weight and cholesterol levels, and exercising. Unfortunately, all these steps may not guarantee that you will avoid heart failure. A virus can strike anyone, regardless of how healthy he or she might be. Or you may be the victim of a genetic predisposition to heart failure, or you may have required a series of blood transfusions related to another medical problem, for example, sickle cell anemia.

In fact, we currently do a much better job preventing other forms of heart disease. Ironically, our preventative success with other heart diseases has funneled an increasing number of people into the heart failure category. The odds are that you've been hearing about more and more people who have been told they have heart failure. Why? Because we've become so proficient at helping people survive heart attacks with the use of clot-busting drugs and devices and surgery. The people who survive one or more heart attacks or have bypass surgery (which is sometimes done even two or three times) are the ones who eventually develop weakened hearts that lead to heart failure. We've statistically increased the chances of the average person falling victim to heart failure; having found effective treatments for many forms of heart disease, cancer, diabetes, and so on, we've simply allowed people to avoid one disease in favor of another. There's nothing wrong with this. If anything, it emphasizes our growing need to focus not only on doing what we can to prevent heart failure but on doing everything we can as early as possible to determine if we have it.

The Asymptomatic Many

The best time to begin treatment for heart failure is before you know you have it. If that seems like a paradox, consider the fact that many people have heart failure for years and aren't aware of it. Just as we can function with one kidney or one lung, we can often function with our heart working at 50% of its normal capacity. I always tell my patients that the good Lord gives us a little extra of everything and that it's not how much heart muscle we have but how efficiently we use it. Although the onset of heart failure can be sudden and can create the same kind of instant trauma as a heart attack, it usually progresses insidiously over a long period of time. During that progression your heart becomes weaker and weaker, though you feel perfectly fine. When the symptoms finally surface, you've already passed an important window of opportunity—the early stages of the disease, which is the optimal treatment time.

We know that if you treat people when they're asymptomatic, the number of times they'll be hospitalized is fewer, the progression of the disease is slower, and the overall survival rate may be higher. Even though you're asymptomatic, you can determine if you're at high risk for heart failure by asking yourself the following questions:

- Have you ever had a heart attack?
- Do you have high blood pressure?
- Are you a heavy drinker, smoker, or drug abuser?
- Do you have diabetes?
- Do you have a family history of heart failure? (Prevailing medical opinion used to be that there is no correlation between heart failure and family history; in the face of mounting evidence to the contrary, that opinion is now changing.)

If you answered yes to any of these questions, you're at high risk; the more yes answers, the higher the risk.

Go to your doctor and tell him or her of your concerns. Depending on many things, including your history and the signs and symptoms you have, your doctor may perform a variety of tests and procedures aimed at determining if you have heart failure and, if so, what form of heart failure you have and what your current status is. These are discussed in Chapter 3.

Telltale Signs

After the asymptomatic stage is the stage in which a person receives early warning signs of heart failure. Again, the faster the following signs are heeded, the better the prognosis:

- Shortness of breath (during activities and/or shortly after lying down in bed at night)
- Fatigue

- Chest pains
- Swollen feet
- Weight gain or loss
- Changes in appetite
- Inability to shake a cold or other relatively minor illness

If you have one or more of these signs, the underlying cause could be any one of a host of things besides heart failure. To enable you to compare your symptoms with theirs, here are some of the descriptions heart failure patients commonly use to express their physical problems: They notice that they can no longer participate in a regular activity or sport without feeling fatigued or short of breath. For instance, golfers complain that they used to play 18 holes without a problem and now get very tired after 9 holes. Some people say they now have to sit down and rest after cleaning one room of the house whereas before they could clean all the rooms without feeling tired. Whether the activity is shoveling snow or walking up the stairs, in all cases people find that they can no longer do what they once did with ease. In many instances, they rationalize the problem rather than consult a doctor. Typically, they attribute their fatigue or shortness of breath to getting older, weight gain, or being out of shape.

Are You Receiving the Right Treatment?

Early treatment is important for many reasons, not the least of which is its potential to control heart failure's impact on the other parts of the body. Since the body is an interactive system, the heart's failure affects other parts of that system, including the lungs, kidneys, liver, brain, and muscles. For example, heart failure often precipitates kidney failure since an insufficient amount of blood is being pumped to those organs; this process is usually insidious but may be hastened by underlying kidney damage from high blood pressure or diabetes. Similarly, untreated heart failure leads to shortness of breath, which in turn makes people inactive and homebound, which leads to a greatly deconditioned state, which usually makes the person even more symptomatic.

If, however, heart failure is treated at an early stage, the damage can be postponed and limited. You may be able to postpone kidney damage indefinitely or for years instead of for months, and you may be able to avoid the poor muscle tone that could turn you into an invalid.

Even if you don't seek medical help in the early stages of the disease, your prospects are probably better than you think. As I mentioned before, not so long ago at least 50% of the people diagnosed with heart failure died within a year of diagnosis. Today, with optimal treatment that percentage has decreased to below 10% for many people—those with good prognostic profiles.

More important, I feel, is the fact that heart failure patients are feeling better and doing more than ever before. Though it's difficult to quantify quality-of-life issues, I've seen a dramatic turnaround in this area: I have patients who formerly would have been bedridden and who now go on ski trips, work regular jobs, and live well-rounded lives. With today's approaches and treatments for heart failure, most patients should be able to make some progress toward feeling better and doing more. If a person has been on a steady decline since being diagnosed with heart failure, he or she may need attention to the typical problem areas discussed in the following paragraphs.

Treating the General Symptoms, Not the Specific Cause

There's a standard regimen of drugs and other treatments that doctors prescribe for heart failure patients. This prescription is fine for a significant percentage of patients but not for a sizable minority. For instance, heart failure can be caused by inflammation of the heart muscle. If a doctor fails to do a heart biopsy, he or she will not learn that this is the problem in a given case and will not prescribe treatment specific to this cause. While treatment for this kind of heart problem remains controversial, many experts think that using certain anti-inflammatory drugs can alter the destructive heart process. Or the doctor might not realize that the patient's condition is a result of a silent heart attack, that the patient has coronary problems that require different medications from the ones he has been prescribing. It's vitally important for doctors to pinpoint the causes of heart failure in their patients so that they can provide optimal treatment.

False Assumptions about Heart Failure

Clearly, when heart failure has been going on for 10 years or more, it's more difficult to reverse all the damage. Someone who has heart failure due to 25 years of severe high blood pressure, for instance, probably has a permanently weakened heart muscle. This person may be helped but probably will never regain complete heart function. But when heart failure occurs suddenly—for example, when it is caused by a virus or is associated with an irregular heartbeat or a pregnancy in a previously healthy woman—it's quite possible to help the patient recover completely. But that won't happen if you're a short-term heart failure patient who's treated like a long-term one. The key to success: your doctor must recognize that the disease has been relatively brief, pinpoint the cause, and tailor the treatment accordingly.

No Reevaluation

Heart function doesn't become static or predictable when a person has heart failure; it's always either getting worse or getting better. When doctors first diagnose heart failure patients, they may grade their condition on one or more "scales" to determine how serious their heart failure may be. They may grade symptoms on a 1-to-4 scale (4 being the worst) and heart muscle function on an ejection fraction scale of 0% to 50% (0% being the worst). These scales can be monitored regularly to detect changes in heart function and to be sure that patients continue to receive treatment that is appropriate. If their condition becomes worse, treatment is changed or intensified. If their condition improves, certain therapies can be eliminated (which may improve the way the patient feels even more).

A Big Bag of Tricks

In many ways, heart failure is a highly individualized disease. The treatment that's right for one person might be wrong for someone else. A slight change in therapy might make all the difference in the world. Fortunately, doctors are becoming more adept at tailoring treatments to patients. We have a big bag of tricks to choose from, some simple and some complex. Some of the things you'll find in that bag are the following:

- Dietary restriction of salt and fluids
- Changing the types of drugs patients are receiving
- Changing the drug dosages
- Using experimental drugs
- Heart transplants
- Experimental surgeries and devices
- Artificial hearts

Though I'll discuss these and other therapies in greater detail in later chapters, let me address a few issues that this list raises.

Many patients often ask, "Why can't I get a heart transplant? My neighbor had one, and it was like a miracle." Heart transplants *can* have miraculous effects. Certainly, the idea of exchanging an old failing heart for a young healthy one is appealing. But heart transplants aren't for everyone. Generally, age 65 is the cutoff for transplants. In addition, people with other medical problems are usually not good transplant candidates (for example, the drugs given patients after the transplant to suppress immune systems can play havoc with insulin-dependent diabetes). Third, the number of donors is limited; there are only about three thousand transplants done annually (see Chapter 9).

Then what about an artificial heart? Again, the idea is appealing, but reality hasn't yet caught up with the ideal. In most instances, artificial hearts are used as "bridges" to transplants; that is, they sustain a patient until a donor heart is available. Though a number of improvements in artificial hearts have been made—there are now small, internally implanted models that don't require huge external machines—they aren't yet the panacea people initially hoped they would be. However, they remain one of the great hopes of the future (see Chapter 17).

One of the more promising experimental surgeries is called a heart wrap, or cardiomyoplasty. This involves taking a muscle from a patient's back, wrapping it around a weak heart, and using a pacemaker to get the muscle to squeeze the heart, simulating the pumping function the heart is no longer strong enough to perform. One of the great advantages this technique has over transplantation is that there's no danger of rejection—the patient's own muscle is being used, not someone else's. As promising as heart wraps are, more research has to be done before they make the transition from experimental to standard treatment.

For now, the best treatments generally involve drugs, dietary restrictions, and exercise. We've made tremendous strides in this area, creating new, more effective medications with fewer side effects and learning how to use them in combination with others to make heart failure patients feel better and live longer. There are many experimental drugs, some of which will probably enable us to take the next great step forward in our fight against heart failure.

How Do You Define Success?

The definition of success in treating heart failure varies and depends on the patient's goals, age, and condition. All patients with heart failure want to feel better and be able to do more. The elderly may have other goals, such as being less dependent on family or neighbors or being able to attend a granddaughter's wedding. For a younger person, an important goal may be being able to get back to work. Certainly, long-term survival is a bigger issue for the 19-year-old than for the 90-year-old. Some patients may want to find out more about what heart failure is and how they can help themselves more.

The pages that follow will help patients achieve these objectives. Success is possible. Though no magic cure exists, it is important for patients to know that numerous options are available that can make a significant difference in treatment effectiveness. Time and again, I've seen heart failure patients who have given up hope prematurely, who have limited their activities unnecessarily, who have suffered needlessly, and who have been denied optimum treatment.

The Importance of Being Optimistic

More than most diseases, heart failure demands patient participation. Patients can impact their treatment by being an acute observer of their condition, by communicating crucial information to their doctor, by following the regimen he or she recommends, and by being optimistic. The last suggestion may sound Pollyannaish, but I've found that optimistic heart failure patients do far better than pessimistic ones. Too often, a heart failure diagnosis becomes a self-fulfilling prophecy: sure that every day is their last, people start acting like they're doomed and treat their bodies like fragile antiques.

Recently, at the request of a cardiologist, I saw a 70-year-old woman with heart failure. He said she was "terribly sick," had been in and out of the hospital, and was now receiving treatments at home. He added that it was difficult for him to convince her and her family to come to my outpatient center to see me; the patient was afraid to be moved and wondered if it was worth the effort. Finally, she agreed to come in, but her family insisted that she come by ambulance.

After her arrival by ambulance, the patient was

brought into my waiting room on a stretcher, with oxygen running, and a somewhat nervous receptionist called me to say my patient had arrived. I examined the patient and found that she was in relatively good shape, that her heart was fairly strong, and that the reason her cardiologist had said she was terribly sick was related to secondary problems that were eminently treatable. I spent 90 minutes with the patient explaining what I had found and the adjustments in treatment that should be made. Finally, I told her that there was no reason for her to be on the stretcher, that she did not need the oxygen, and that she could help herself by beginning to walk more and more each day. I had her walk around the room, and she was both amazed and delighted that she could do so. Since her son was in the waiting room, I suggested to her that she walk out of my office on her own two legs to meet him, which she did.

A few minutes later another doctor came in, shaking his head. I asked him what was the matter. "The receptionist," he said, "just told me something that I thought you'd appreciate. She said, 'I heard Dr. Silver was good, but I've never seen anything like that. A woman comes in almost comatose on a stretcher, with oxygen, and a little while later she walks out with a bounce in her step and a smile on her face.'"

Certainly, I hope this book helps you live longer. But just as importantly, I hope it puts a bounce in your step and a smile on your face as you find success with heart failure.

Chapter 3

Evaluating Your Condition

Many heart failure patients possess either erroneous or vague or even *no* information about their condition. Not only do they underestimate or overestimate its seriousness, but they often don't know the specific cause of their heart failure and don't comprehend how it developed and how it evolved. We doctors are to blame, in part, for this situation. For too long we've lumped all heart failure patients into the same category. We don't admit that heart failure is a relatively unexplored medical territory, and instead of telling patients we don't know we sometimes make unfounded guesses and inadvertently communicate the wrong information. Even today some physicians betray their fatalistic attitudes about the disease, sending false messages to patients that there is no help or hope.

Considering the advances we've made in heart failure diagnosis and treatment, there is no reason for doctors to continue these practices. For both psychological and treatment reasons, people need an accurate assessment of where they stand as heart failure patients. Psychologically, patients require accurate information to deal with their disease; sometimes just knowing what caused it can remove some of their anxiety. I truly believe that people want to know the details. From a treatment perspective, patients benefit from knowing the cause, type, and stage of their heart failure; we're in a much better position to improve patients' quality of life and help them battle the disease if they are informed participants in their treatment.

Let's examine several classification systems for heart failure and the diagnostic methods available to patients and see what they can reveal about an individual's condition.

Functional Classification

A classification system based on patient symptoms was developed years ago. Called the New York Heart Association Functional Classification, it divides heart patients into four categories:

- Functional Class I: Asymptomatic; Patient is not short of breath or fatigued with any activity.
- Functional Class II: Patient is short of breath or fatigued after moderate activity (such as climbing two flights of stairs, golfing nine holes, or carrying a load of wash up from the basement).
- Functional Class III: Patient is short of breath or fatigued even after very mild exertion (such as walking across the house or up half a flight of stairs).
- Functional Class IV: Patient is exhausted, short of breath, or fatigued when just sitting still or lying down in bed.

While there are data to suggest that even a simple classification like this can help determine how a heart failure patient may do in the future, relatively few physicians use this functional classification system on a routine basis.

Diagnostic Tests

Ejection Fraction

One of the most important measurements we take, which serves both as a baseline measurement and as a means of following a person's progress, is of the *ejection fraction*, which is the amount of blood the heart ejects or pumps with each contraction. The normal ejection fraction for the left side of the heart is approximately 50–60% and 45–55% for the right side. Obviously, there is a gradation, but anything below 25% suggests an unfavorable prognosis. A measurement of about 35% or higher offers a much better prognosis of long-term survival. (Note, however, that this is quite variable: someone at 37% may not do as well as someone at 15% or 20%!)

Three methods exist for measuring ejection fractions, and each makes the measurement differently. To get more information and enhance the reliability of the diagnosis a doctor may use two or more of the methods.

When these tests are complete, patients can be fairly certain of the accuracy of both the left and right ventricle ejection fractions. If your doctor fails to perform one or more of these measurements, you should ask why so that you can understand how your doctor is evaluating your degree and type of heart failure.

Cardiac Catheterization. In *cardiac catheterization* (left ventricular angiogram), contrast material or dye is injected into the left ventricle of the heart, which allows the measurement of the shape and volume of the heart. On the plus side, this method provides a relatively accurate measurement of the ejection fraction by calculating the volume of blood in the heart just before the heart squeezes and the volume after the heart has squeezed out all it can with a single beat. On the minus side, it's an invasive measure that carries a small degree of risk.

MUGA Test. In a *MUGA* (multiple gated acquisition) *test,* or *RNA* (radionuclide angiogram), a small dose of radioactive material is injected into the bloodstream and a scanning machine then tracks this material, revealing how much blood is ejected out of the heart, much like a cardiac catheterization. One of the best attributes of this test is that, with certain modifications and if requested by the doctor, it can also measure the ejection fraction of the right ventricle. Typically, the left ejection fraction receives more attention, since the majority of heart failure patients have problems there, but we've found that the right ejection fraction is often a very good predictor of a patient's survival and that it complements rather than duplicates the prediction made by the left ejection fraction.

Echocardiogram. The *echocardiogram,* another noninvasive procedure, bounces sound waves off the heart to provide an ejection fraction reading (among other important measurements of the heart). Though it's helpful in revealing enlarged hearts and in determining whether the problem is primarily diastolic or systolic, it may not always provide good visualization since the echo beam has to pass through various structures in the chest. Also, it can over- or underestimate the ejection fraction. However, if a good heart image is obtained, this is a very useful test, since it can often give good information about heart valves, the sac that envelops the heart, called the pericardium, and even what the pressures are within the heart and lungs—all noninvasively!

Treadmill Testing and Cardiopulmonary Exercise Testing

Since one of the most common manifestations of heart failure is shortness of breath as people move about or exert themselves, one of the best ways to see how symptomatic they really are is to put them on a treadmill and have them exercise. This of course has been done for years to see if people with coronary artery disease develop chest pain or changes in their electrocardiogram. Also, treadmills are used to make sure the drugs we use to treat coronary artery disease or high blood pressure are working.

One of the surprising facts to emerge from exercise testing with heart failure patients, however, is that there is very little relationship between the number of seconds or minutes a person with heart failure can walk on the treadmill and his or her overall survival. Nonetheless, many patients with heart failure commonly get a treadmill test, and this may be an important part of the screening process to determine the cause of the heart failure and to get a rough idea of how symptomatic an individual is. Treadmill tests are often combined with other procedures that take a picture of the blood flow to the heart, such as a thallium scan.

Aware of the limitations of the regular treadmill in terms of prognostic ability, doctors have increasingly turned their attention to a more specific way of looking at how the heart and lungs work together to provide blood and oxygen to the remainder of the body. This is still another form of exercise test, which I will describe in just a moment. First, let me review an important concept.

As I mentioned before, we all have a little extra heart function, so people can have their ejection fractions drop down to half of normal and may still not notice any change whatsoever at rest or with minimal activity. However, since one of the key symptoms of heart failure is exercise intolerance, it is when people start to do things—walk, work, exercise—that they notice difficulties. Because the measurements of ejection fraction are done at rest, they often give little useful information about how limited a person may be with exercise. (Sometimes we can do exercise MUGAs or exercise echocardiograms to get this information.) Also, since the heart must pump blood through an extensive network of blood vessels to get it to the muscles to do the work of walking, lifting, and so on, it is important to test how the heart, lungs, blood vessels, and muscles all work together during exercise to really determine how patients use what they have in terms of heart function. ("It's not what you have but how you use it," I often tell patients.) One of the best ways we can do that is with a cardiopulmonary exercise test (CPX), which checks the heart's and lungs' ability to deliver blood and oxygen to muscles. By measuring peak oxygen consumption, which reflects the maximal amount of blood the heart can pump to the tissues, we can obtain a very accurate and reproducible measure of a heart patient's condition. The big problem with this measurement is that the particular exercise testing equipment needed for it isn't widely available. Aside from a few heart failure specialists and universities, most doctors don't have access to this equipment. Until cardiopulmonary testing equipment becomes more readily available, this valuable test cannot be routinely offered to many patients.

There are other exercise measurements available; many physicians are currently using a 6-minute walk test (the ground the patient can cover in a total of 6 minutes) to help fill the gap when CPX testing cannot be done. This seems to have some proven reliability for heart failure patients. I feel, however, that the CPX is the superior measurement.

Stress Hormone Test

A simple blood test will reveal your stress hormone, or plasma *norepinephrine*, level. This hormone, which is normally released during periods of stress, helps you cope with powerful emotions by causing the heart to pump stronger and faster. When your heart muscle weakens, your body senses that loss of strength and your stress hormone level goes up and stays up. Years ago heart failure expert Dr. Jay Cohn conducted a study that revealed that patients with high plasma norepinephrine levels had a markedly greater chance (80%) of dying within 2 years than did patients with near-normal levels, the 2-year mortality rate dipping down to less than 20% for patients with a normal level. The stress hormone test remains one of the important prognostic indicators or "guesstimators" for heart failure.

Biopsy of the Heart Muscle

We use a heart muscle biopsy (endomyocardial biopsy) when we suspect *myocarditis* (inflammation of the heart muscle) or when we need more direct evidence about the condition or status of the heart muscle than indirect testing offers. Though some physicians don't do biopsies because they believe the risk outweighs the reward or feel the yield is low, I've found that biopsies are very useful in certain situations, yielding information that would be difficult to find without direct access to the heart muscle. In a number of instances, I've found conditions that other tests failed to reveal—sarcoid of the heart, for instance, which is a special kind of inflammation in the heart and one for which specific treatment is available that can markedly improve the patient's condition. The stated risk for a biopsy is .1%, a risk I feel is even lower when the biopsy is performed by someone very skilled in this procedure.

Other Medical Tools

The *electrocardiogram* and chest X-ray are well-known medical tools that provide a variety of useful information for heart failure patients. Electrocardiograms may reveal whether someone has had a heart attack, and can detect irregular heartbeats (either causing or being caused by heart failure), congenital defects, problems with the lining of the heart, and other data. A chest X ray helps determine the heart size, the degree of congestion, the presence of pneumonia or blood clots in the lungs, and the *cardio-thoracic ratio*, that is, the amount of the chest cavity in its transverse diameter filled by the heart. The normal ratio is less than 50%. A heart that fills a greater proportion of the chest cavity signifies an advanced stage of heart failure. Often, a person has heard that they have an enlarged heart and may think that this means a heart that is stronger than normal, since an "enlarged" arm muscle would probably be a stronger one. Generally, however, an enlarged heart muscle is overstressed or damaged and usually works less efficiently than a normal heart muscle. Any disease which causes heart failure may also cause an enlarged heart and, in fact, many doctors use the term as a euphemism for heart failure. Occasionally, an enlarged heart can mean a heart that is thicker than normal due to high blood pressure, and, again, this is not necessarily a more efficient heart muscle. Sometimes, a well-trained athelete may have an enlarged heart that functions normally, or even supernormally, but this is the exception to the rule.

Rather than just recording a patient's heartbeat for a few minutes in the office, physicians can use a continuous recording of heart beats, or 24-hour Holter, to spot abnormal pauses or extra heart beats. In recent years cardiologists have learned that some people may even develop a form of heart failure because they have a higher than normal number of heartbeats. In some instances, when medicine reduces the heartbeat rate to a normal level, the heart failure is ameliorated or may even disappear.

Pieces of a Puzzle

Other diagnostic tests exist—sedimentation rate, serum sodium, and so on—but we've covered the major ones. As a rule of thumb, the more tests a doctor does, the greater his or her ability to provide patients with an accurate diagnosis and effective treatment. This does not mean the more tests the better. It simply means that when doctors base their conclusions on only one test, they run the risk of jumping to erroneous conclusions. For instance, doctors who receive test results showing a very low ejection fraction may tell their patients that they don't have long to live. The problem, of course, is that their one measurement may be inaccurate or that they have incorrectly diagnosed the cause of the low ejection fraction (the true cause may be treatable) or that their patients may still be able to use their heart function well, meaning that their exercise capacity may be terrific.

While multiple tests can help confirm one another, they can also create a new problem: conflicting messages. For instance, an ejection fraction may be nearly normal but the stress hormone level may be alarmingly high. It's not uncommon for conflicting results to exist, and doctors can often resolve these conflicts based on other input. They can also use additional information to confirm a suspected problem or to adjust treatment for increased efficacy.

Patient History

Questions to Determine the Presence of Heart Failure

In addition to our high-tech tests and equipment and despite the fact that the heart is not the most accessible of organs, doctors can gather a startling amount of valuable data by examining and talking to patients. "How do you feel?" is one of the first and most important questions a doctor can ask you. Your answer can go a long way toward determining what test might be needed or resolving conflicting tests and determining the most effective treatment. Therefore, never hide the truth about how you feel. Many times patients put up a tough front and insist they haven't been feeling ill when they really have been. Or they over-dramatize problems because they possess other agendas— they want to get out of work or garner sympathy. The patient history is crucial for heart failure patients; it contains subtle clues as well as obvious facts that clarify or confirm test results. In the paragraphs that follow are some of the questions your doctor may specifically ask about your symptoms as well as the rationale behind the question.

Do You Have Chest Pain or Pressure? Your doctor may ask you if you feel pain or pressure in your chest, as well as in your neck, back, or throat. This symptom may indicate problems with the coronary arteries, but it can also occur with some types of heart valve problems, in *hypertrophic cardiomyopathy* (a condition where the heart muscle becomes too thick), or even with thickening of the heart due to high blood pressure. If you do have this symptom, the doctor will ask further about where the pain or pressure is and will want to know what brings it on, what makes it better, if it moves around, and how long it lasts.

Do You Have Shortness of Breath? Your doctor may ask if you have shortness of breath, how long this has been noticed, what brings it on, what makes it better, and whether there are other symptoms that go along with it, such as chest pain or sweatiness. Commonly, patients allow this symptom to progress over weeks to months to years and only seek medical attention when there is a marked limitation (unable to go out of the house without getting short of breath, for example).

In addition to shortness of breath as you move about (we call this *exertional dyspnea*), there may be shortness of breath when you lie down on your back (*orthopnea*) or shortness that occurs in the middle of the night that awakens you with a feeling of suffocation or coughing (*paroxysmal nocturnal dyspnea*). Both of the latter result from the extra fluid that accumulates within your body and that gets back into the bloodstream when you lie down and take the force of gravity off your legs. This extra volume of blood puts an extra load on the heart, and the weakened heart forces the extra blood up into the lungs; the extra blood there causes poor oxygenation in the lungs, and the person becomes short of breath. Usually, the seated position helps, as does a walk around the room or a trip to the bathroom. Also, people who experience this symptom may place extra pillows under their head, so don't be surprised if the doctor asks about how many pillows you use at night. Getting rid of extra urine at night (*nocturia*) is also related to the nighttime return of fluid to the heart and then the kidneys, so you will be asked about this as well.

Are You Having Problems Sleeping? A sleeping problem may be related to lung congestion or to frequent nighttime urination. However, it often is related more to frequent naps or dozing off and less physical activity during the day, which means that there is less need for nighttime sleep. We also think a great many of our patients have difficulty sleeping because of concern—or even some depression—over their medical condition. It is common to see one or more of these factors preventing a normal sleep pattern. Often, when the heart failure improves and a person can get a single good night's sleep, his or her whole perspective and outlook on life improves as well.

Are You More Fatigued Lately? Fatigue is simply one of the many manifestations that the heart is not doing its job as a pump of blood. The muscles and even the brain may not get enough blood or enough oxygen, which is the fuel the body operates on, and this will result in fatigue. People commonly attribute fatigue to being out of shape or getting older, since it can sneak up on a person slowly over the years. Fatigue after even minimal activity can cause a person to doze off easily or catnap frequently during the day. This can lead to poor sleep at night and can start a vicious cycle of confusion of days and nights (day-night reversal).

Have You Gained or Lost Weight Recently? With heart failure there is usually a decline in the appetite, and weight loss may occur. More commonly, however, there is accumulation of fluid in the body due to the poor heart function and the person notices weight gain despite eating almost nothing. The fluid accumulation may be noticed in the hands (rings are tighter) or in the feet (the person may switch to wearing looser shoes or tennis shoes); or it may simply be that clothes (skirts, dresses, pants) that used to fit are now tight. Obviously, many conditions can cause weight loss or gain, but, surprisingly, this may be the first thing a person or a family member notices. I started treating an elderly woman recently because her daughter, who provided all her meals and therefore knew how little she really was eating, noticed that none of her clothes fit anymore. Since the elderly woman was relatively inactive, shortness of breath was really not one of her initial complaints.

Have You Noticed Changes in Your Appetite? Most commonly, people with advanced heart failure notice a loss of appetite. They describe a bloated feeling or a feeling of filling up fast after eating very little (we call this *early satiety*). People who would consistently take second or third helpings can now barely finish half the food on their plate. The reasons for this are many but include more inactivity; the high energy costs of digesting food, which a person with a weakened pump can't afford; swelling of the intestine, from the extra retained body fluid or blood; and swelling of the liver, for the same reason, which leads to the liver enlarging and pressing on the stomach so that the stomach's capacity is reduced.

People with these problems should be told to eat smaller, more frequent meals and foods that are easier to digest. Once the initial fluid overload is reduced with proper treatment, this problem often disappears rapidly for many people.

Do Your Legs Ever Swell?   Swelling of the legs is a finding that can represent a variety of causes and does not always reflect a form of heart failure. When it is related to the heart, it can start out as just a little tightness at the ankles at the end of the day, after standing for most of the day. Later it progresses to a swelling that remains even in the morning and then to swelling that encompasses the entire body, including a marked swelling of the belly (even the genitalia may become swollen when this condition is severe).

Questions Following a Diagnosis of Heart Failure

Now let's review some of the more important questions doctors ask once a diagnosis of heart failure has been made and the relevance of the answers to diagnosis and treatment.

How Did Your Heart Failure Begin and at What Age? What Were the First Symptoms, and How Did They Evolve?   To more precisely characterize a patient's heart failure, the doctor will want to know what the patient's first symptoms were, when they began, and how they developed. Here are some typical responses to this line of inquiry and what they mean to the doctor:

A 60-year-old man notes that he has had high blood pressure since he was 40, began feeling "sluggish" in his fifties, and had his first episode of heart failure at 58. He says, "My internist checked my heart and said it was fine." On the basis of this history, I would suspect that this man has hypertensive heart disease, that he started out with a diastolic abnormality, and that he may now have systolic and diastolic abnormalities.

Another man responds that he had his first heart attack at 40, another one when he was 52, and a third at 55. He complains of swollen legs and feeling winded and tired since the third attack. It's likely this man is suffering from ischemic heart disease; that is, his heart failure is a result of multiple injuries to the heart muscle due to blocked coronary arteries.

A woman complains that her episodes seem to have "come out of the blue." She says she feels fine during the daytime hours but at around 11 at night, after being asleep for about an hour, she finds herself gasping for breath; her husband has had to call the paramedics. This woman is probably suffering from *flash pulmonary edema*, which means the sudden backup of blood from the heart into the lungs, which causes severe lung congestion. This could be a result of diastolic dysfunction or perhaps coronary disease and/or hypertension.

These brief case histories are simply examples to show you how the symptoms you tell your doctor really are the guideposts he or she will use for determining further testing and treatment. Besides describing the symptoms, you should communicate to your physician when they began, how long they've been going on, and whether they appeared suddenly or gradually. When you tell your doctor about your symptoms, you may be doing nothing more than confirming what he or she already suspects. But you may also be giving your doctor that nugget of information that allows him or her to make the right decision about your treatment and to give you an indication of how sick (or how relatively healthy) you are.

What Other Medical Problems Have You Had in the Past? Heart failure specialists are alert to those diseases, symptoms, and medications that may have caused or exacerbated a patient's current condition or that may be a valuable clue for diagnosis and prognosis. Some of the red flags are diabetes; thyroid condition; viral illnesses; coronary disease and related factors (smoking, high blood pressure, high cholesterol); drug and alcohol abuse (or even just use); and kidney disease. For instance, the heart failure patient who reports that she had a viral illness preceding her symptoms of heart failure may be the victim of myocarditis (heart muscle inflammation). Sometimes the link between a previous medical problem and heart failure may be more subtle. A middle-aged woman recently came to my office after experiencing her first heart failure episode. After taking her medical history, the cause of her condition was still a mystery to me until she mentioned that she had had Hodgkin's disease almost 30 years before. It turns out that she had received relatively high doses of radiation and that the radiation had damaged her heart muscle and coronary arteries. Suspecting that she might have radiation heart disease, I ordered specific tests and was able to help her considerably.

Has Anyone Else in Your Family Experienced Heart Failure? Most people realize that coronary heart disease runs in families, but until recently the same link wasn't established for forms of heart failure. Though there is some debate over this issue, my experience has been that dilated cardiomyopathy often runs in families.

What Do You Do for a Living, and How Do You Feel at Work? Though it might not appear to be relevant at first blush, occupations can reveal a great deal about a heart failure patient's condition. When patients start talking about specific activities in the workplace (from walking to the office, to putting products on shelves, to loading trucks, to running to catch the train), they frequently remember to relate a physical problem they've been experiencing there: "Doctor, I've noticed recently that whenever I start erasing the blackboard, I feel dizzy and winded." Any upper extremity activity can trigger heart-related pain or shortness of breath, and people generally clearly remember when such a symptom first began at work, thus giving doctors a time line to chart the onset of the disease. Of course, patients may first become aware of such a symptom when it relates to some physical activity in the home as well. I've had patients relate their symptoms to such things as washing dishes, washing their hair, and performing housework. This type of information also gives doctors a benchmark against which they can measure how patients fare after treatment. The doctor will want to know if the patient still feels winded when erasing the blackboard (or loading the truck or stocking the shelves, etc.), or if the feeling is gone or lessened.

The environment in which a patient works can also contribute to a diagnosis. Certain airborne chemicals or dusts can contribute to heart failure problems. In addition, people who work in cold environments (very cold rooms or outside in winter) experience more heart failure symptoms than do people in warm environments. This is because cold causes blood vessels to constrict, which increases the heart's work load. I've seen patients for whom a change in environment results in a near-miraculous improvement in how they feel.

Physical Exam

Heart failure often manifests itself in surprisingly visible, audible, and tactile ways. The following paragraphs describe some of the signs doctors look for when examining heart failure patients.

High Blood Pressure

Hypertension over a period of years does more than contribute to coronary disease; it also weakens the heart. Unfortunately, many heart failure patients never realize they have high blood pressure. Part of the problem is the prevalent attitude in the medical community that moderately high blood pressure is acceptable, particularly in the elderly. The common notion that your blood pressure should be 100 plus your age is an absolute myth and one that should be destroyed. Years of moderate hypertension can lead to heart failure in people in their forties and fifties and is a common cause of heart failure in people over 65. While we generally say that blood pressure should not exceed 140/90, this does not mean that our goal should be 139/89! In many countries where salt is not a major dietary substance, normal blood pressure is 90/60 for life. Normally, the top number (systolic blood pressure) should be between 90 and 120, and the bottom number (diastolic blood pressure) between 60 and 80. Ask your doctor for more specific details.

Rapid Resting Heart Rate

When the body senses heart failure, the heart responds by beating faster. Resting *tachycardia*, or fast heartbeat of 90 or 100, especially if it stays at that high level for a period of time, signals a serious problem. At rest the heart rate normally slows. The actual rate depends on age, the status of the heart, and the individual's overall level of conditioning. Generally, a resting heart should beat 50–70 beats per minute. You can check your heart rate by feeling the pulse in your neck or wrist, or by listening to the heart with a stethoscope. An ECG will also measure heart rate.

Unusual Skin Color and Abnormalities

Cyanotic, or blue, skin suggests a form of heart failure that can be due to a congenital defect; also suggests a lung problem that can ultimately cause a special kind of heart failure known as right-sided heart failure, or *cor pulmonale.* A fingertip or fingernail examination (checking for color, shape, or appearance changes) can reveal some circulatory causes, while some skin lesions can indicate an esoteric form of heart failure, such as that related to scleroderma or lupus erythematosus.

Congested Lungs

Lung congestion may mean that the heart is weak and that blood has backed into the lungs. Blood normally flows from the right side of the heart, through the lungs, into the left side of the heart. If the left side of the heart becomes weakened, however, blood flow may reverse in part and back up, or congest, the lungs. When there is too much pressure back up, more fluid leaks into the lung tissue and may cause a cough, shortness of breath, or even a feeling of suffocation. In these situations, doctors call what they hear when listening to the lungs with a stethoscope *rales* or *crackles.*

"Raised" Neck Veins

Neck veins are to the heart as a dipstick is to a car. They help monitor how much fluid is inside the circulation. If there's too much blood and pressure builds up on the right side of the heart, the neck veins become swollen or engorged. We primarily look at the internal jugular vein, but we can look at other veins of the body to give us some clues to the "volume status" of the person. This tells us how much extra blood or fluid is within the circulation.

Abnormal Heart Sounds

Listening to the heart through a stethoscope placed on various areas of the chest can reveal a murmur, which means abnormal blood flow; extra sounds, which may indicate a weakness; or "rubs," which reflect extra fluid accumulating around the heart.

Swelling of Various Body Parts

Swelling may be seen in the abdomen; in the back (*presacral edema*); in the arms, legs, or feet; or even in the genitalia. Swelling in the liver can be palpated. Usually, this swelling, which is caused by the retention of excess fluid and salt, affects the entire body, but it may be best detected in one specific area or another. For example, a person with leg swelling usually already has liver swelling, and so on, but he or she may not be aware of this liver swelling until the leg swelling is appreciable.

The More You Know, the Better Off You'll Be

Knowledge is power. These tests, exams, and questions have a cumulative value for both patient and physician. The information gleaned from this process provides patients with a much better understanding of the condition. I've found that patients need that understanding.

TABLE 3.1. Heart Failure Type, Causes, and Diagnostic Tests

Heart failure type	Cause	Diagnostic test
Ischemic cardio-myopathy	One or more heart attacks	Angiogram (heart catheterization); stress echocardio-gram
Hypertensive cardio-myopathy	High blood pressure	Blood and urine tests; echocardio-gram
Dilated cardio-myopathy (id-iopathic cardiomyopathy)	Unknown	Possibly endo-myocardial biopsy; echocardiogram; angiogram
Valvular cardio-myopathy	Either congenital or acquired valve damage	Echocardiogram; car-diac catheteriza-tion
Cor pulmonale	Emphysema or other causes of lung tis-sue damage	Echocardiogram; Swan-Ganz cathe-ter measurements
Hypertrophic cardio-myopathy	Genetic or result of spontaneous de-velopment	Echocardiogram

They have an innate desire to know the cause of their heart failure, what their prospects are, how advanced the disease is, what can be done, what the alternatives are, what they should expect, and what their obligations and duties are. Table 3.1 summarizes the types of heart failure, their causes, and the tests used to diagnose them.

From a treatment perspective, these data are essen-tial. Contrary to myth, heart failure is treatable and, in some cases, reversible. A battery of tests and questions may help us identify those people who are suffering from reversible forms of heart failure. Though these people are in the minority, they still comprise a significant percentage of heart failure patients. Instead of assuming their condition will get progressively worse, and treating them accordingly, we can look for the sometimes subtle signs that indicate a reversible problem, for example, an inactive or too active thyroid gland.

We've gained so much knowledge and made so much progress with drug and other therapies that it would be a shame to waste those accomplishments because we've misdiagnosed heart failure patients or failed to acquire the necessary information for effective treatment. The SAVE study, a recent study of people who had heart attacks, reinforces this point. The study divided its subjects into two groups: Those who received medications to prevent progressive heart enlargement and weakening, and those who didn't. The study concluded that the medicated group had much less enlargement and a significantly lower rate of heart failure than the nonmedicated group. Yet in spite of this clear demonstration of the value of such medication, many heart attack survivors who never have another heart attack die prematurely from heart failure because no one has monitored their heart size or treated them for this problem.

The more we know, the easier it is to tailor treatment for a specific heart failure patient, that is, to treat our patients holistically. We can determine, for instance, if a patient is in New York Heart Association Functional Class I, II, III, or IV (with I being the least serious). If we know someone is in Class IV, we would probably design an aggressive treatment regimen; perhaps we would consider experimental approaches and use higher doses of medication. For someone in Class I, on the other hand, we might be much more concerned about the day-to-day quality-of-life issues and might therefore try to reduce medications and diuretics to a minimum.

Finally, our ability to predict the specific cause of heart failure death can also aid in our treatment approach. On the basis of the tools discussed in this chapter, we can often determine that a given heart failure patient is most vulnerable to death from one of the following: (1) progressive heart failure (the majority of patients die because of the progressive weakening of the heart muscle); (2) arrhythmia, a series of irregular heart beats; (3) one of a variety of more unusual causes, such as a blood clot that embolizes and enters the lungs. If, for instance, we can determine that you are most likely to be victimized by arrhythmia, we can try drugs or implant a defibrillator, a device that senses an irregular heart beat and automatically delivers an electrical shock that restores a normal beat. Defibrillators have been found to decrease mortality rates for heart failure patients. Defibrillators are generally used when the heartbeat is too fast, in contrast to pacemakers, which prevent the heartbeat from becoming to slow.

Chapter 4

How Attitude and Emotion Affect Heart Failure

When patients hear the term *heart failure*, they are frequently devastated. The word *failure* has an ominous ring, and many people automatically assume, "This is it; there's nothing left to be done." They may even sink into a deep depression from which they never extricate themselves.

There have been studies that demonstrate a link between the mood and physical condition of patients with various diseases, and empirical evidence leads me to believe that such a connection certainly exists for heart failure patients. Time after time, I've seen optimistic, positive-minded patients feel better and live longer than pessimistic, negative-minded ones. I'm not sure why this is so. Perhaps the correlation is similar to that between stress and heart attacks—studies have demonstrated clearly that stress is a risk factor for heart disease. Or it might be that the heart is an organ exquisitely attuned to our emotions, that the folklore about people getting "heartsick" because of a lost love has more truth to it than we think.

Whatever the reason, a positive mental attitude is

therapeutic. In this chapter, I'd like to explain why this is so and how patients, physicians, family, therapists, and support groups can combine their efforts to foster this attitude.

The Negative Attitudes

Fear, anger, denial, and depression are some of the understandable reactions to a heart failure diagnosis. Fear of the unknown is a natural response. Patients are afraid of the myriad tests and treatments they face; of the reactions of friends, family, and employers; and their own mortality. We commonly see anger in dilated cardiomyopathy patients. They've avoided bad habits such as smoking and maintaining a high-cholesterol diet and have never had high blood pressure, yet their hearts are failing; the injustice causes them to strike out. Another possible response to the diagnosis is denial. Patients who use denial insist that they're fine and give their doctor misleading signals about their condition. They insist to others, and perhaps even to themselves, that they can "tough it out." Finally, there's depression, probably the most common emotional response to a diagnosis of heart failure and the most destructive. Depressed patients convince themselves there is no hope, and such a conviction can become a self-fulfilling prophecy.

In many ways these responses mirror the traditional grieving process. Acceptance of their condition doesn't come for many patients until they've worked through these and other emotions. Sometimes there's a false acceptance initially, usually by patients who have been suffering for years and who now feel better as a result of treatment. A diuretic can quickly and effectively relieve excess fluid, bringing comfort to patients, but it may not improve their heart function. Because they feel so much better, these patients may then indulge in a high-salt diet or discard their medicine; they assume that they have improved sufficiently to cheat on their regimen and that their doctor can bail them out again if necessary. When their symptoms grow worse, the seriousness of their situation hits them for the first time.

I've found that heart attack survivors are often especially bitter when they learn they have heart failure. They may have assumed they were well after a successful coronary bypass and only learn later that the trauma of the heart attack has weakened the heart muscle to the point where it's failing.

Depression, anger, and other negative emotions harm treatment in two ways. First, patients stop doing what they should be doing or resume habits they should give up. They don't take their medicine (or take it only sporadically); they ignore salt, fluid, and other dietary restrictions; they miss appointments with their doctors or fail to provide them with accurate information about their symptoms; they fail to get proper exercise and are no longer active and involved; and they continue bad habits like smoking or drinking.

The second problem is that when patients give up in their minds, they also frequently give up in their bodies. It's as if they're sending a signal from their heads to their hearts that it's not worth the effort. This mental surrender combined with the practical problems caused by not following a prescribed medical regimen can shorten life and destroy quality of life.

To avoid this situation or remedy it, patients, physicians, nurses, and family must understand how and why heart failure patients often become so pessimistic and depressed. Many times, certain factors make a bad situation worse.

Common Catalysts

Sleep deprivation can make healthy people moody and irritable; the effect on people with heart failure can be even more severe. Heart failure patients often have trouble sleeping at night for the following reasons: some experience fluid backing up in their lungs and therefore have difficulty breathing; those taking diuretics wake up frequently at night to go to the bathroom; and some have an often unarticulated fear that if they go to sleep they won't wake up.

Certain drugs patients take can sometimes exacerbate negative emotions. Possible side effects of heart-related drugs include mood swings, confusion (especially in elderly people), altered taste sensations, and problems with balance and gait. A drug such as an ACE (angiotension-converting enzyme) inhibitor can create a nagging chronic cough. Diuretics often cause the mouth to be dry and make people feel they must limit their activities because of frequent trips to the bathroom.

Perhaps the most depressed people are those with the greatest change in functional capacity, namely, vigorous men and women who worked and played hard and who have been told (or have decided on their own) to quit work and "take it easy." For many men, especially, the inability to work and the corresponding economic hardship are crushing blows. One of my patients is an insurance salesman in his early fifties with kids to put through college. Because of his heart failure, he lost his job (it requires a great deal of energy to make sales calls, and his primary symptom is fatigue). Ironically, he also lost his insurance coverage, which adds to the economic pressure he is experiencing.

Idle time often allows patients to dwell on their conditions and symptoms. We see patients who never complained about anything in their lives suddenly become filled with self-pity. Feeling a loss of independence is a major problem as well. Often this is unwittingly fostered by well-meaning spouses, doctors, and nurses who try too hard to reinforce restrictions on the patient's diet and activity.

Finally, the loss of sexual function can radically alter patients' moods. Poor blood flow to sexual organs and certain medications can result in impotence or a decrease in pleasure. More often than not, though, this condition is psychological rather than physiological. Nonetheless, the damage has been done, and both men and women suffer from moodiness because of this loss.

Fortunately, we've developed a number of successful tactics to combat these problems. Let's examine what these tactics are and how doctors and patients can use them.

Getting Off to a Positive Start

What doctors tell heart failure patients during their initial meeting has a tremendous influence on patients' attitudes. It's very easy for people to jump to conclusions and to think their condition is far worse than it really is. Because patients are usually quite upset, they can easily misinterpret or fail to understand what their doctors tell them. I've also found that some physicians inadvertently emphasize the negative over the positive, telling patients only what's wrong with them.

Individuals with heart failure don't improve unless they see the possibility for improvement. They won't take their medicine and will ignore fluid and salt restrictions if they think they only have a few months of low-quality life left. That's why if there's a chance for improvement—and there usually is—patients should be aware of it. In almost every case, I'm able to tell a patient during the first meeting, "I think there's something I can do for you."

I also ask a very simple question: "If I could help you do something you either can't do now or are worried you won't be able to do, what would it be?" The responses run the gamut—from playing golf, to going back to work, to attending a grandchild's wedding. Setting goals is crucial. They give patients reasons for living and nonmedical barometers to measure how they're doing. Many times, when people surprise themselves and achieve that first goal, they're motivated to reach the next one. If Mary finds that she is able to walk around the block, she'll be willing to work toward the goal of walking to the store by herself. Or, if a person can gradually go back to work part-time, there is hope that he or she will eventually go back full-time or realize that part-time work is suitable and acceptable. Even a brief visit to relatives or a trip to a shopping mall gives the patient hope that he or she is not permanently housebound.

When I've determined the specific condition of a heart failure patient and clearly communicated it to him or her, I then create short-, medium-, and long-range treatment plans and explain each one. This takes the mystery out of treatment and transforms a scary and uncertain future into something more structured and understandable. At the same time, I outline the treatment options associated with each plan. Too often, patients give up hope when treatment option number one doesn't work; they assume such an option was their best and last hope. They don't realize that there are usually many other options with equal chances for success.

Simple Treatment Adjustments

Treatment plans shouldn't be set in stone. Even if a change in treatment won't significantly improve a patient's condition directly, it may do so indirectly; when patients feel better, they're more optimistic about life, and that optimism motivates them to do everything possible to get better.

Of course, no medically related change should be made without carefully evaluating a patient's condition. Treatment plans for some people must maintain a delicate balance; for them, even the slightest variation can have serious repercussions. For most patients, relatively minor changes do little harm and can do much good. I've found that the following adjustments can make a world of difference in the emotional well-being of heart failure patients:

Vary the Times for Taking Diuretics

Many patients become sleep deprived because diuretics cause them to wake up a number of times at night to go to the bathroom. Others are embarrassed at work, or afraid to go to work, or even skip doses because of worries about incontinence. Taking diuretics at more convenient times can eliminate or lessen these problems. In some cases, the doses can be decreased. I've also found that, for certain people, diuretics work better in the afternoon than in the morning. If the morning diuretic is causing problems at work, the patient may be better off taking it only in the afternoon.

Ease Up on Dietary Restrictions

Restrictions must make common sense. When the limits doctors place on patients regarding eating and drinking are too numerous or too strict, they can negatively and significantly alter their moods. One of my patients came into my office a few weeks after he'd been limiting his salt intake to under 2 grams daily and said, "I've been feeling much better, but you've made my life miserable." It turned out that he loved ketchup almost as much as life itself, and he was really upset about not being able to put it on his food. Allowing him to have a little ketchup now and then significantly improved his outlook. Many times, I've found that simply telling patients not to add any salt to their food from a salt shaker reduces their salt intake to an acceptable level. For others, there are one or two key dishes that need to be avoided (see Chapter 11). I would say that most family disagreements regarding treatment for heart failure center around dietary restrictions.

Vary Dosages and Brands of Drugs

Even minor variations in the dosage or brand of drug used can produce a change that helps the patient begin to succeed. For example, if a patient gets a cough with one of the ACE inhibitor drugs, then he or she should get the cough with all the various brands of these drugs. However, I frequently switch brands trying three or even more, and, surprisingly, many people end up on the needed drug without a cough! We should also not overlook the placebo effect. A study recently at Ohio State University proved that the placebo effect, or the belief in a patient that a pill may help, actually did improve heart function in heart failure patients.

Maintain Rather Than Limit Activities

If you take away a person's job, hobbies, exercise routine, and family and social life, what does he or she have left? Every physician should determine what activity is important to a patient and do everything possible to help him or her continue that activity. A significant percentage of heart failure patients are remarkably active. Some recent studies have demonstrated that progressive exercise therapy can actually improve cardiac function and in fact is one of the important treatments for this condition (see Chapter 10). In my experience and that of my colleagues, active, participating patients do much better than passive, disinterested ones.

Support Groups and Therapy

Given the millions of people diagnosed with heart failure, you would think that there would be a correspondingly large number of support groups for those patients and their families. Unfortunately, that's not the case. Relatively few groups exist (see Appendix II), and those that do are highly specialized. Young Hearts, for instance, is a group originating in Chicago for people under 40 with heart abnormalities. And while there are heart transplant support groups, these organizations, as the name implies, exclude anyone who hasn't had or isn't waiting for a heart transplant.

Having started the first heart failure support groups in Chicago, I saw the tremendous psychological benefits they offer group members. The ideal support group serves two purposes: (1) it brings in experts (for example, doctors, nurses, nutritionists) to answer practical questions about heart failure, and (2) it allows members to exchange common concerns and experiences. As a result, people no longer feel they're alone and helpless; they enjoy the camaraderie that develops and the opportunity to share their feelings with people who have a similar diagnosis and who therefore understand in ways that others cannot.

Family and friends can form another type of support group. They can help the heart failure patient look forward instead of backward, and they are able to ameliorate the bitterness and anger that mitigate against successful treatment. From a purely practical standpoint, they can help patients deal with what is often a confusing regimen of pills, doctor appointments, and dietary restrictions. By helping patients get used to a new routine (which pills to take and when, for instance), they enable them to achieve a comfort level in those crucial first few weeks.

Some patients require more help than support groups or family members can provide, or they may not have access to support groups or family. Psychological counseling is an option a patient should consider and the physician should recommend when a patient's negative state of mind is interfering with his or her treatment. Seeing a psychologist, social worker, or psychiatrist can be very helpful, especially when a patient is acutely depressed. At the same time, however, therapy can be expensive and may not be covered by insurance. In the case of the heart failure patient who is only mildly depressed or the one who is extremely worried about money, strong support is needed from friends, family, professionals, and, occasionally, short-term drugs that help the depression without worsening the heart muscle function.

Societal Attitudes

Society can make heart failure patients feel like second-class citizens. A patient of mine who was in excellent shape after a transplant experienced numerous job rejections and told me she felt like an ex-con. Primarily because of worries about insurance costs, companies are wary of hiring anyone with a diagnosis of heart failure. Insurance companies hear the term "heart failure" and run the other way, even without knowing about or listening to the objective assessment or prognostic indicators. Similarly, there are relatively few support groups and rehabilitation programs tailored to heart failure patients' needs because of the false assumption that there's nothing to be done for these people. Is it any wonder that heart failure patients feel depressed?

My hope is that as more and more people are diagnosed with heart failure, organizations and institutions will change their attitudes and create supportive programs and policies. Such programs and policies can go a long way toward improving the outlook, that is, both the prospects and perspective, of heart failure patients.

Chapter 5

Doctor–Patient Relationships
How to Find and Work with the Right Physicians

Patients' interactions with their doctors can have a tremendous impact on their treatment and quality of life. While this statement is true for any illness, it is especially relevant for heart failure patients and their physicians because of the disease's chronicity. Because patients with heart failure rarely have just a once-a-year checkup, they need the kind of relationship with their physician that can endure the ups and downs, the periods of feeling better and the periods of feeling worse. There may be multiple office visits but, hopefully, few hospital visits. Therefore, a good relationship between patient and physician is crucial. In many ways this relationship is much like a good marriage: it must be prepared for the long haul and must be based on mutual appreciation, trust, working together, honesty, and, most of all, communication. Poor communication in this disease can mean the difference between success and failure.

My goal in this chapter is to provide patients with the information they require to choose the right physician, be alert to difficulties in the patient–physician relationship, and identify their own responsibilities. I want to show them how to get the best treatment they possibly can by establishing good communication with their doctor. To help you understand how all this can be accomplished, I'm going to walk you through the process that takes place when a person is first diagnosed with heart failure.

First Contact

In this country only 17% of all patients with heart failure get their care from a cardiologist. *And this is how it should be!* Since heart failure is so common, the majority of patients are cared for by primary care doctors (doctors in family practice, general practice, or internists).

Many heart failure patients enter the system complaining to their primary care physician about such seemingly vague symptoms as fatigue, lethargy, and shortness of breath. Doctors typically respond in a variety of ways depending on how they interpret the symptoms and the findings of the examination. They may start with blood tests that come back as normal. Frequently, doctors attribute symptoms to the aging process and do little else. Sometimes fluid congestion in the lungs is thought to be asthma or pneumonia. Even if there is a history of coronary disease in a patient, doctors frequently focus on the short-term goal of preventing a heart attack and ignore the long-term possibility of heart failure. In many instances, aging truly may be the sole cause of the symptoms, and in other cases preventing a heart attack correctly should take priority over preventing heart failure. The problem, however, is when heart failure symptoms are overlooked, misdiagnosed, or ignored, causing a patient to suffer needlessly when there is so much that can be done today.

It's possible that your doctor has correctly diagnosed heart failure but is not doing everything possible to maximize your treatment. The question arises as to when you should ask to be referred to a cardiologist, a specialist in internal medicine who has received additional training in cardiovascular disease. I would say that in general you should consider contacting a cardiologist or ask to be referred to one if

- You don't respond to treatment, that is, if your symptoms don't improve or become worse, or if you have had multiple hospital admissions for heart failure
- You're diagnosed with heart failure but your physician can't pinpoint the cause
- You are at risk (see Chapter 2) and have symptoms you think may be related to heart failure but heart failure has not been mentioned as a potential cause
- You're increasingly limiting your activities because of heart failure
- You've been diagnosed as having mild heart failure and perhaps are not taking any medications (Our current thoughts are that even very early symptomatic patients benefit from some medical therapy).

Cardiologists and Other Specialists

All cardiologists are not alike, and simply seeing a cardiologist does not mean you will get better or more advanced heart failure care. It is interesting to see that, owing to the major increase in the incidence of heart failure and the need to reduce health care costs, heart failure is getting more and more attention by professionals, hospital administrators, news reporters, and politicians alike. I recall even a couple of years ago going to give grand rounds lectures on heart failure to physician groups of not more than eight or ten people (half of whom were asleep!). Now, interest has increased, there's better attendance, frequently there's a hospital administrator present, and the questions go on forever! Nevertheless, since heart failure has been around forever, there is a general feeling that we know all there is to know already. That is why I feel treating heart failure is like an avocation—you either love treating heart failure or you don't. I feel that an interest in heart failure translates into more concern, more attention to detail, and better care.

The point is that cardiologists don't have a lock on interest in heart failure. In fact, I have seen terrific interest and skill in treating heart failure in recent years, having been exposed to some of the excellent primary care physicians in our community. A cardiologist whose interest is in something other than heart failure, such as catheterization or balloon angioplasty, may not be as aggressive in treating heart failure. Also, while professional journals, videos, and meetings provide a great deal of information on the newer treatments for heart failure, what is taken up and used is very dependent on interest. My advice, therefore, is to continue to search until you find a physician with an interest in you and an interest in heart failure. If your primary care doctor wants to refer you to a cardiologist, again you should ask the same questions: "Will the cardiologist have an interest in me and does he or she have an interest in heart failure?"

It's also possible that other specialists will be involved in your treatment. Sometimes other organs or conditions become involved with heart failure. The following items list the specialists who are most likely to be called upon and why:

- Kidney specialists (*nephrologists*) may be asked to give advice on how to improve kidney function or even to do dialysis (cleaning of the blood by a machine). Kidney problems may be due to diabetes, drugs, aging, or even to heart failure itself.
- Diabetes specialists (*endocrinologists*) may be consulted on how to better control diabetes, which commonly involves kidney and heart problems, including heart failure; often, better control of the diabetes can improve heart failure symptoms and vice versa.
- Lung specialists (*pulmonologists*) may be consulted because the heart and lungs really work as a single unit. Many patients have both heart failure and lung problems, such as emphysema, lung cancer, or pneumonia. Even more commonly, the heart can cause lung problems (wheezing, congestion), and at times lung problems can directly affect the heart (right-sided heart failure or cor pulmonale).

Shouldn't Every Heart Failure Patient Have a Heart Failure Specialist?

Heart failure patients don't necessarily need a heart failure specialist, and even when they do, it's not always possible to get one. Primary care physicians and cardiologists may do a fine job of taking care of heart failure patients, even if they're not specialists in heart failure. It all depends on their level of interest! If the cause of the failure is relatively easy to determine and treat, if the progress of the failure is slowed or arrested, and if the patient feels better, then a specialist probably isn't needed.

Too often, however, heart failure doesn't follow this ideal scenario. The cause can be difficult to track down, and effective treatment can require a fine balance of medications and other measures. Heart failure specialists, because of their training and experience, are in the best position to orchestrate all this. They're also probably in charge of an experimental drug or treatment research program, one that may prove helpful to patients who haven't responded to conventional treatment.

Unfortunately, there are in this country relatively few true heart failure specialists, that is, cardiologists who spend 100% of their time working with heart failure patients. In fact, if you ask your primary care doctor for a referral, he or she might not be able to provide one. In small towns, especially, you won't have much luck (you may even have difficulty finding a cardiologist). But even in major metropolitan areas, you might not have any luck. You may want to contact the local hospitals that have heart transplant programs, but even at such hospitals there is no guarantee that you will find a dedicated heart failure specialist with access to new and investigational treatments.

Doctor–Doctor Communication

Because more than one physician is usually involved in a heart failure patient's treatment, coordination of effort is imperative. If one doctor is unaware that another has changed a patient's medication, the result can be a potentially life-threatening situation. A delicate balance of medication, diet, and other factors is necessary, and while one physician should be in charge of maintaining that balance, all health care professionals need to work together effectively.

The primary care physician is often in the best position to oversee the patient's care, to act as the quarterback of the team, even if a heart failure specialist is involved. A family doctor can monitor treatment in light of the patient's history and is able to establish a baseline against which the patient's changing condition can be measured. He or she can also take care of secondary problems associated with heart failure—urinary tract infections, colds, diabetes—that cardiologists often are unable or unwilling to address. Finally, the primary care physician can provide a long-term perspective on the patient's prior medical conditions, home life, and other physical or emotional issues, as well as communicate with other doctors and family members, keeping everyone in the information loop regarding a change in the patient's treatment or condition. I cannot overemphasize the importance of a good primary care doctor; I personally insist that patients keep or try to establish a relationship with a family doctor.

Doctors' Roles and Patients' Roles

Whether you've chosen a cardiologist or a primary care doctor to treat your heart failure, that physician should be a combination of Sherlock Holmes and Ronald Reagan. In other words, he or she should be an excellent investigator and a good communicator.

One of my patients once told me, "I like you because you seem like you're a good detective." A detective is an appropriate analogy, since heart failure specialists must search and probe not only for the cause of the heart failure but for the most effective treatment. Because there are so many different causes of the disorder and subtleties of treatment, a good heart failure physician is constantly looking for something revealing or for a new and better approach.

Communication, too, is a valuable commodity. I've found that what sometimes helps heart failure patients the most isn't a fancy drug or procedure but simply information. I've had patients who come to me complaining about how terrible they feel admit that they aren't limiting their salt or fluids. When I ask them why they aren't limiting these things, they respond, 'My doctor never told me to." Doctors sometimes assume that patients know more than they do. Communicating clearly what patients should and should not do greatly facilitates treatment.

The doctor–patient relationship, however, isn't a one-way street. I'm always chagrined when I see patients who absolve themselves of responsibility for their treatment, who tell me they don't know which medications to take because their spouse or someone else always tells them. Psychologically and physiologically, patients benefit from assuming responsibility not only for their medications but for as many aspects of their treatment as possible. They should ask for an explanation of an unexpected new symptom and should proactively tell their doctors when another doctor changes their medication.

Patients should come prepared when they meet with their doctors. That means making sure the doctor has all medical records or can gain access to them, bringing their medications with them to their appointments, and keeping a diary of medications taken and symptoms noticed.

Adapting to each other's interpersonal style is a project for the patient and the physician. For instance, my style is to talk to patients, examine them, write some notes, review previous records, think intensely about their problems and decide what else to do or try, and then discuss my decisions with them. At the end of the office visit, I ask if there are further questions and make sure they don't need any prescription refills. Until patients figure out my style, they think I will bolt out of the room before they get a question answered or a prescription written. So, inevitably, they keep on talking when I'm doing my thinking. After a few visits and my explaining about my thinking period, I am accorded more silence. (It's funny how silence in a doctor's office is very uncomfortable for most people.) Other details, like the best time to call the doctor or to ask questions during an examination or how to schedule appointments and get prescription refills, are a matter of getting used to each other.

Heart Failure Patients' Questions

One of the most important things a patient can do is come armed with a list of questions. Too often, patients leave the doctor's office without getting the answers they need. To prevent this, I've created two lists of questions to share with you. The first contains questions heart failure patients most frequently ask, the second questions that are often on their minds but aren't asked either because they're too embarrassed to ask them or because they're not sure how to articulate them. Because of the uniqueness of each patient's situation, no answers to these questions are offered here. Instead, the lists are meant as an introduction to dialogue between patient and doctor.

Most Frequently Asked Questions

- When can I return to certain activities (sports, for instance)?

- When can I go back to work?
- What activities, foods, and other things do I have to limit?
- Should I exercise and, if so, how much?
- Can I take my water pill early in the day?
- What is the intended effect of this medication?
- What side effects should I expect?
- Why is this test being done?
- What are the alternatives to this medication (or test)?
- What should I do if I forget or skip a medication?

Unasked Questions That Should Be Asked

- Am I doing myself harm when I get short of breath?
- How will my condition affect my sex life?
- How long am I going to live?
- Is this disease transmittable to my children?
- Is this given procedure going to hurt?
- Does my insurance cover this procedure (or drug)?

There are many more questions for each list, depending on the patient and his or her particular situation. Whatever the questions are, you should make sure you pose them to your doctor. Write a list at home and take it with you. No matter how stupid or embarrassing some of them might seem, don't be afraid to ask. Not only are the answers important for the heart failure patient's mental well-being, but the questions enable patients to communicate their concerns to their doctor. I have actually seen a feeling of great calm come over my most anxious patients who come in with a long list of questions; as we go through the list and answer each question, the patients realize they are being listened to and understood.

Summary

In summary, there is no absolute right doctor to care for your heart failure, but the doctor should be someone with more than a passing interest in heart failure. If you're not making progress or are even getting worse, ask your doctor for a referral or seek out a specialist. Remember, you will, hopefully, have a very long-term relationship with whoever cares for your heart failure. Also, since you may have to rely on him or her to help you with very serious decisions (taking experimental drugs, undergoing surgery, gong on kidney dialysis, or getting a heart transplant), pick a good communicator as well. Be a good communicator in return, and allow yourselves time to learn each other's individual style. Those are critical steps toward success with heart failure.

Chapter 6

Heart Attacks and Heart Failure
What's the Difference?

People frequently confuse coronary disease (blocked arteries that can lead to heart attacks) and heart attacks with heart failure. Either they use the terms synonymously or they inextricably link them. While coronary disease is a common pathway to heart failure, it does not always lead to it. And obviously you can have heart failure without ever having had a heart attack. To make the connections and distinctions clear, let's examine coronary disease's impact on the heart muscle.

"Time Is Muscle"

When arteries are blocked with cholesterol and blood platelets, little or no blood flows through the artery to the heart muscle. When the muscle doesn't receive blood, chest pain, also known as *angina*, results. When such pain is prolonged, it usually means that serious damage is being done to the heart muscle and, if not quickly reversed, a heart attack will ensue. This prolonged period of pain is the prelude to a heart attack, since blood is being denied to the heart muscle. The sooner the blockage is cleared with a clot-busting drug on a catheter or a balloon, the less the damage to the muscle and the lower the risk of a heart attack (thus, one drug company's slogan: "Time is muscle").

The more damage done to the heart muscle, either through repeated tiny attacks of angina or from one or more heart attacks, the more likely it is that the patient will experience heart failure. Though it's difficult to pinpoint the exact amount of damage that guarantees the progression to heart failure, most doctors agree that around 40% (that is, 40% of the left ventricle, which is the main pumping chamber of the heart) is the point of no return. The percentage is cumulative: it does not matter whether it's 40% damage from one heart attack or 25% from one, 5% from another, and 10% from a third. So it's possible for the interval between a person's first heart attack and the beginning of heart failure to be months or even years; the person might not reach the 40% figure until a third or fourth heart attack.

The 40% damage might come not only from the actual heart attack. Often multiple or repeated attacks of angina can cause heart failure. There are other factors that in combination with a relatively mild heart attack can push people into the heart failure category, including the following:

- Diabetes mellitus
- High blood pressure
- Prolonged angina episodes (which can scar the heart muscle)
- Medications (examples of drugs that may have a negative effect on heart muscle function are verapamil, metoprolol, and flecainide)

- Bypass surgery (The problem is that bypass grafts can close over time without doctors or patients realizing they've closed. This can be a painless process causing a silent heart attack, which still weakens the heart muscle. Since the majority of bypass grafts close within 10 years of the procedure, this is a common problem.)

Limit the Damage

Heart attacks don't have to progress to heart failure. If you can keep the damage under 40%, you can postpone or avoid failure. To do so, however, requires a keen awareness that you're not out of the woods simply because you survived a heart attack. In many instances, a bypass or other procedure and drugs may cause you to feel great, and your heart function may be excellent. You feel so good that you start repeating the behaviors that caused your heart attack—smoking, drinking, a high-fat diet, no exercise, stressful activities. Then you have another heart attack, but this time the muscle is damaged beyond the 40% limit and heart failure symptoms develop.

Until recently, doctors focused on helping patients overcome the acute condition of a heart attack but did not have reliable means for helping to prevent the development of heart failure. Many times, this translated into the wrong choice of medications: drugs were given to patients that actually weakened their heart (but relieved the pain associated with coronary disease). Or physicians recommended no medications for patients who had relatively minor heart attacks. But a recent study shows that even people who have suffered small heart attacks experience heart enlargement if they don't receive appropriate medication. Enlargement weakens the heart and increases the chances of failure. Early use of these medicines (for example, captopril) may prevent or delay the development of heart failure for many heart attack victims and may even decrease the amount of damage.

Lowering the Percentage of Damage

One of the great discoveries made by Dr. Dean Ornish and other cardiologists is that coronary disease can be reversed. This is good news for coronary disease victims and even better news for prospective heart failure patients. If you've experienced 20% or 30% damage to your heart muscle, you're perilously close to heart failure. But if you can reduce the risk of another heart attack, you've taken a big step back from the precipice.

Also, the thinking goes that if 20% of the muscle is damaged, perhaps half of that, or 10%, is not irreversibly damaged but is, instead, "hibernating." That is, the metabolism of the heart has slowed because it isn't receiving sufficient blood; it has become very "quiet" in order to protect itself. But if you restore the blood flow, this 10% can "wake up" and be healthy muscle again. We've found that even if a patient experiences 40% damage, some of that damaged muscle function can be restored.

The key, therefore, is to remove blockages and start blood flowing to the heart as quickly as possible after the heart attack. A cardiologist recently told me that he was doing an electrocardiogram (EKG) on a patient at the hospital when the patient experienced huge changes in the EKG, signaling a heart attack. The cardiologist immediately moved the patient to the heart catheterization lab; the artery where the blockage was seen was identified, and the blockage was removed. Three days later this patient underwent an aggressive exercise test, and his heart function was perfectly normal; whatever damage there was had been minimized or quickly reversed, and the patient's risk of heart failure was greatly reduced.

Determining Your Risk

Ischemic heart disease, or heart attacks, is one of the worst pathways to heart failure. Compared to other heart failure patients, those with a history of heart attacks generally have a poorer prognosis, feel worse, and are more likely to succumb to sudden death. Typically, these patients are also more vulnerable to arrhythmia (irregular heartbeats) than are others.

Given all this, it's important to do everything possible after a heart attack to determine your risk for another one. Although that second attack may not do as much damage as the first and you may survive it, the cumulative damage could nudge you into heart failure. Before you leave the hospital, therefore, your cardiologist should "stratify" your risk for a subsequent heart attack. This can be done by using a variety of tests, including an echocardiogram and Holter, MUGA, and treadmill tests, as well as by determining what kind of heart attack you had. In addition, patients who complain of chest pain after the initial attack tend to be more vulnerable than others.

If you're at high risk for another heart attack, your doctor should be very aggressive in his or her treatment, that is, in finding and removing blockages, prescribing appropriate medications, and designing strict diet and exercise regimens. Since there is a common link between heart attacks and heart failure, aggressively limiting the severity of damage done to the heart by coronary artery disease can help to weaken that connection and even possibly sever it.

Chapter 7

Conventional Treatments for Heart Failure

In this chapter I would like to outline some of the conventional or standard treatments for heart failure that are being used today. These are common procedures or medications that can or should be applied to most people who have heart failure. Obviously, how many of these treatments are applied to any one individual depends on the seriousness of his or her heart failure. In addition to the prescribed medications, other treatments, like dietary restrictions, can and should be explained thoroughly, if not by the doctor then by the nurses, dietitians, or office staff involved with caring for the patient.

Salt Restriction

I recently saw a middle-aged gentlemen who had come to see me at the recommendation of another cardiologist. After I had taken the initial part of his history, it was clear that the patient had a fairly advanced case of heart failure. A quick glance at the medications he was taking indicated that his fine cardiologist had already given him most of the conventional medications he should have had. The patient had been through a very elaborate series of tests, and every bit of information to be known about his diagnosis had already been determined. Finally, I turned to the patient and his wife and began to ask them about sources of sodium that might be in his diet. With heart failure the heart's ability to pump blood is impaired, and the body senses this as not having enough blood in the circulation (see the section on diuretics later in this chapter). This stimulates the body to retain salt with the goal of retaining even more fluid. Obviously, then, eliminating the salt in the diet is one of the very first steps in helping to reduce the excess fluid that may accumulate in the body. In fact, when we discuss diuretics, or water pills, you will see that their primary task is to first clear salt out of the body and that the water then tends to follow.

This patient at some point had been told to restrict the salt in his diet, but he had not been given detailed instructions about this. He told me that he did not add any extra salt from the salt shaker, but when I reviewed several of his favorite meals, it became clear that he was getting loads of salt in seemingly innocent ways. For example, one of his favorite treats was to go to a local restaurant where they had "home-cooked soup and a terrific salad bar." What more could a cardiologist ask for? he thought. Unfortunately, the tasty home-made soup was loaded with salt, and the patient did not realize that the salad bar that looked so great was sprayed with a sodium-containing preservative to help keep those fruits and vegetables looking fresh. And his favorite house dressing would have sent the salt police into a tizzy! Additionally, all of the canned vegetables he was using were high in salt, and he was unaware of the high salt content in most of his other condiments. The final blow came when he told me about some frozen dinners he frequently consumed, all under a terrifically healthy-sounding name, but when I went and got a sample box for him to look at, it turned out that practically each one of those meals contained 1,000 milligrams of salt, more than half of what his total daily intake of salt should have been (see Chapter 11). One of our heart failure nurses spent 45 minutes with the patient and his wife instructing them on how to pick foods that have a lower sodium content. I think it came as a tremendous shock to them that despite all the husband's medical therapy his treatment was inadequate because he was not controlling the salt in his diet, something that was well within his power. When I saw this patient about 2 weeks later, he was feeling remarkably better, yet I really hadn't done a thing to treat him.

Sodium restriction, then, is critical. The degree of restriction is individualized, but I generally tell my patients not to exceed 2 grams of salt a day. Unless you are used to eating heavily salted foods, this in fact is fairly liberal, and you can learn to enjoy food with this sodium restriction. Basically, I follow the 2-gram limit because that is what most patients learn in the hospital; also, if I tell them more than 2 grams, they tend to exceed that limit, anyway. I tend to be a little less strict with those patients who do not have a serious problem with fluid retention, but I do insist on some sodium restriction on virtually everyone. The following analogy illustrates the point I'm making here: if you are going to build a beautiful home, it makes no sense to put thousands of dollars into building and decorating it unless you have a solid foundation. The same applies to treating patients with heart failure: patients can be on every drug in the book as well as on every experimental medication, but their heart failure won't get better unless they adhere to the basic rules, which include salt and fluid restriction. All too often I think we doctors assume that patients are getting specific information about salt restriction from either the nurses or the dietitians, and that may or may not be true. Furthermore, although patients have been told about salt restriction in the past, they need to hear it again and again and in commonsense terms. One patient told me that he was aware that he was supposed to be on a 2-gram sodium diet, but then his next question was, "What is a gram?" Patients are frequently too embarrassed or intimidated to ask for specific information, but they must have this information. There is a wide variety of good information out there: in books, in magazines, and in publications available from your local chapter of the American Heart Association.

Finally, patients always ask me about salt substitutes. By and large, I think that these are acceptable, but you have to be careful because some of the salt substitutes are, in fact, potassium salts instead of sodium salts. Very high levels of potassium in the diets can be as serious a problem as high levels of sodium. My best advice is this: Learn to eat a restricted sodium diet, and you and your heart failure will be better for it.

Fluid Restoration

The other cornerstone in the treatment of heart failure is fluid restriction. Again, since one of the primary problems with heart failure is excess fluid in the body, which the heart must pump to the kidneys to get it out of the body, then it makes sense that the smaller the volume of fluid going in, the less work there is for the weakened heart and the less congestion there will be in the body.

However, I think it is common to find patients who have severe heart failure and who are taking all kinds of medications but who have never once been told to restrict the fluids in their diet. In fact, when I ask patients about restricting their fluids, I've had many quite proudly announce, "Oh no, doctor, I try to drink as much water as I can each day!" I think we have all heard since childhood that it is wise to drink plenty of fluids. Unfortunately, I must tell patients that this is terrific advice as long as they don't have heart failure. Once they understand that they need to restrict fluids, controlling the heart failure is often amazingly simplified.

The same sorts of problems come up with fluid restriction as with salt restriction: since there are multiple hidden sources of fluid, we try to make sure that patients count the fluid of their soups, juices, coffee, tea, and soft drinks—even the water they drink to help them swallow their pills (some patients who have heart failure take so many pills that this can be a considerable source of fluid). Once again, the amount of fluid restriction depends on the individual case, but by and large we tell most patients to limit fluid consumption to about $1\frac{1}{2}$ to 2 quarts a day.

Some patients need to be stricter than others, and for some the 2 quarts can be liberalized. My experience is that most patients tend to underestimate how much fluid they are actually drinking. Many patients who come to see me with refractory heart failure end up on the same medications that were prescribed for them before—or even on less medication—simply by becoming believers in fluid restriction. We've had success with many different methods of keeping track of this 2-quart limit, but perhaps none is as successful as the following system, which a patient of mine invented. Basically, at the beginning of each day he filled up a 2-quart container with water. Each time he drank some fluid, he poured that same amount of fluid out of the container. He told me that when the container was empty, he stopped drinking for the day.

Perhaps the most severe complaint I get from my patients who go on fluid restriction is that their mouth is dry. This, of course, is due to the fluid restriction as well as the water pills they are already taking. If your doctor feels you can do with a little more fluid or a little less diuretic, appropriate adjustments can be made. There are many tricks I teach my patients so that they can learn to live with the fluid restriction and thereby live better with their heart failure. Some of the things I commonly recommend to my patients to help them keep their mouths moist and maintain the fluid restriction are the following: chewing gum, popsicles, sucking ice cubes or chips, small sips of water (instead of big gulps!), and hard candies. Frequently brushing your teeth is also helpful.

Conventional Drug Therapies

For many years doctors have relied on a couple of simple medications to help control the symptoms of heart failure. While the treatments used for many other diseases in medicine have changed dramatically from those used 50 or 100 years ago, many of the heart failure treatments have remained the same. The primary reason for this is that these treatments do work, at least in terms of relieving some of the symptoms that patients with heart failure have.

The three common drugs considered the core treatment for the heart failure patient today are (1) the diuretics, or water pills; (2) digoxin; and (3) a group of medicines called angiotensin-converting enzyme inhibitors, or ACE inhibitors. Digoxin has been used for hundreds of years whereas the clinical use of ACE inhibitors has only spanned the last 10 years. Interestingly, there is more clinical information proving the safety and efficacy of the ACE inhibitors than there is for the diuretics and digoxin. Nonetheless, the use of drugs like the diuretics and digoxin are so ingrained in the treatment of the patient with heart failure that virtually every patient who needs them gets put on them routinely. This, unfortunately, is not always the case for ACE inhibitors. Perhaps because of their newness or because of a doctor's lack of familiarity with recent medical studies on ACE inhibitors, it is estimated that up to 70% of patients who should be on these drugs are not! In the following paragraphs I discuss a little bit of the rationale for the use of each of these agents, including some of the pros and cons your doctor will weigh when deciding whether or not to use these medications for you.

Diuretics

To understand why we use diuretics in treating patients with heart failure, you must first understand one of the important ways in which the body responds to a decrease in heart function. During our evolution we have carried with us the so-called homeostatic mechanisms, which are reactions that help keep our biological processes as stable as possible. Our body homeostatic mechanisms were probably developed to respond not to heart failure but, rather, to sudden losses in blood flow, for example, from having been attacked by a prehistoric carnivore. What the body, primarily the kidneys, then senses is that not enough blood is getting to it, and it sets in motion, in an attempt to restore the body to stability, a series of events that cause the body to avidly retain salt and fluids.

Unfortunately, when a person has heart failure and not enough blood flow gets to the kidneys, the same mechanism is set into action, and fluid and salt are again avidly retained. This is one of the first steps in setting up the vicious cycle of heart failure: the increase in fluid and salt in the body only serves to weaken the heart even further, which in turn decreases the blood flow to the kidneys even more, which means that more fluid and salt are retained, and so on.

Diuretics, or water pills, simply address the problem we have just discussed. That is, with heart failure the patient retains excess fluid and salt, which overload the blood vessels, organs, and tissues of the entire body. Water pills attempt to clear the extra salt and water through the kidneys and thus rid the body of some of the extra fluid that it is retaining. Now this is not quite as simple as it sounds. Water pills are prescribed for a variety of situations: for example, they are one of the commonly recommended treatments for high blood pressure as well as for the fluid retention many women encounter in the premenstrual period. In such settings, where the patient has normal heart function along with normal kidney function, the diuretic can frequently produce a "super" effect (and those who have taken a diuretic know what I mean; you feel as though you are spending the entire day in the washroom!). For many patients with heart failure, however, the results are not the same: if the heart function is too weak to deliver enough blood flow to the kidneys, the diuretic's action may be minimal or absent. Therefore, there has to be at least some preserved cardiac pumping function in order to get the blood flow to the kidneys so that the kidneys can create urine adequately; only then can a water pill aid the kidneys and help clear the excess fluid.

Another problem is that kidney function may already

be impaired; frequently, the kidneys are operating at only 15% to 25% of normal. This may be due to the many years of heart failure, where there was impaired blood flow to the kidneys, or to an underlying disease such as long-standing high blood pressure or diabetes mellitus, which may be in part responsible for the heart failure as well. In that situation the effectiveness of the water pill is going to be diminished, and increasingly larger doses of water pills have to be used. When patients retain fluid and have leg edema, or leg swelling, they are actually retaining fluid everywhere in the body, including the lining of the stomach and the intestines. We forget that when we take a pill, it has to go down to the stomach and intestines and be absorbed through the linings of these organs and work its way into the bloodstream before it can ever do its job. Excess fluid in the lining of the stomach and intestines prevents or decreases the absorption of many medications, including water pills themselves. Some patients will notice that their water pills seem to work exceedingly well on certain days and less well or not at all on other days; this has a lot to do not only with the amount of blood flow to the stomach and intestines but with the amount of swelling in the lining of those organs. When water pills taken by mouth produce no effect, the patient needs to be either seen in the office or hospitalized in order to get an intravenous dose of the diuretic medication, which goes right into the bloodstream and bypasses the absorption phase.

The oral water pills nevertheless are one of the basic medications we employ, to a greater or lesser degree, in most patients who have some form of heart failure. In certain forms of heart failure (for example, in diastolic dysfunction, such as hypertrophic cardiomyopathy, or in forms of valvular heart problems, such as aortic stenosis) diuretics should be used with caution or not at all, since they can worsen the situation rather than improve it. While the general trend is to give increasingly larger doses of diuretics as heart failure progresses, other medications can be added to help limit these dosages.

There are a number of common side effects that occur with diuretics (see Chapter 8). Although their intended purpose is to help wash out some of the blood salts and minerals along with excess water, they can do so over-zealously in some patients, which may result in dehydration as well as in severe electrolyte (such as sodium, potassium, or magnesium) deficiencies, which in and of themselves can cause symptoms and can put the patient at increased risk for irregular heartbeats and worse heart function. Aside from causing electrolyte abnormalities, diuretics can wash out calcium, which can lead to weakened bones, and can precipitate deposits of uric acid into the joints, which can cause an attack of gout. Because of these potential problems, it is frowned upon to have the patients themselves regulate the amount of diuretic medication they take.

By and large, the benefits diuretics produce outweigh the potential side effects, and most patients usually feel better when the excess fluid in their body has been cleared away. The use of diuretics has to be explained carefully to patients so that they understand what the medication is supposed to be doing and do not interpret the excess urination as an undesired effect. It is important to get an idea of what the patient's day is like and to try to schedule the diuretic doses around the person's daily routine. For example, if a person has an hour's train ride to work each morning with no washroom facilities on the train, taking the diuretic first thing in the morning might not be the wisest choice. Similarly, if diuretics need to be taken twice a day and the patient waits until bedtime to take the second dose, he or she can forget about a good night's sleep. The sleep deprivation just leads to a vicious cycle of agitation, insomnia, and perhaps even serious changes in a person's disposition and mood. That is why I usually recommend that the second dose of the day, when needed, be taken just after the patient returns home from work in the afternoon. That gives the diuretic time to do all of its work and leaves patients more "dried out," if you will, so that they can get a good night's sleep. It is not uncommon for me to find within the first week or so of beginning treatment with a patient that simply rearranging the medications to fit the lifestyle allows the patient his or her first good night's sleep in several years. Ignorance by a doctor of a patient's routine can frequently lead to lots of missed doses of a diuretic, with the patient remaining edematous and symptomatic and the doctor concluding that nothing more can be done for the patient. Usually a happy medium can be achieved so that the diuretic doses get taken and patients do not totally disrupt their lifestyle.

The bottom line in using diuretics is for the patient to understand what the goals are and what potentially serious as well as seemingly trivial side effects this kind of medication can produce and for the doctor to prescribe the diuretics in a way that ensures their optimal use in the patient.

Digoxin

Digoxin is a medicine that has been available for over 200 years. Yet, surprisingly, we are still learning how it works in heart failure and what its potential advantages are. It has been used primarily for two main purposes in treating patients with heart failure. Digoxin acts within the heart muscle to improve its contraction and therefore the pumping action of the heart. Digoxin is also commonly used in patients who have irregular heartbeats, such as atrial fibrillation, which can cause the heart to beat too fast. That is, digoxin can slow the heartbeat or even help it become more regular.

While digoxin is a very old drug, this does not necessarily mean that it is a completely safe one; in fact, the side effects from it are fairly common. In the use of digoxin we say that there is a narrow "therapeutic window," which means that the dosage has to be adjusted very carefully; if too little is given, there is no effect, and a little too much can actually cause bad effects and make a patient even worse. Probably because of the need to carefully adjust the dosage, as well as the lack of any study demonstrating that digoxin has a favorable effect on the mortality rate in heart failure, this drug has had a slight decline in popularity over the past 10 years. However, two very recent studies found that heart failure patients who were taken off digoxin for purposes of the study suffered a major decline in how they felt and that more of them required hospitalization for recurrent bouts of heart failure. There is currently under way a large study sponsored by the National Institutes of Health that we hope will reveal the impact of digoxin on mortality rate in patients with heart failure.

I think in many ways we are getting smarter about knowing when to use digoxin as well as when to be cautious in its use. For example, since much of the drug is cleared out of the body through the kidney, those with poor kidney function, such as the elderly, may accumulate the drug and suffer more side effects. Also, since we can now more easily measure the level of digoxin in the blood, we can be alert to a high level and reduce the dose. Similarly, we find that some patients are taking a dose that is too low for them and that simply increasing the dose can give them some help for their heart failure.

Unfortunately, digoxin interacts with many other drugs that are commonly used in heart failure. In fact, the absorption of digoxin can be altered by other drugs and even by the foods we eat. (The day after Oprah Winfrey had a guest on her TV show explaining how certain foods affect the absorption of medicines, I got a rash of phone calls from patients who wanted to be sure I was aware of the fact that oat bran could significantly decrease the absorption of digoxin. I took this as a positive sign that many patients are taking more responsibility for their own health care.)

I think the important point to remember about digoxin is that while it is an old-fashioned remedy, it is commonly being used today in over 70% of patients who have heart failure; up until about a decade ago digoxin, along with diuretics, was truly the mainstay of therapy for patients with heart failure. I think in the next 5 years or so we will learn a great deal more about this superb remedy for heart failure.

Vasodilators and Angiotensin-Converting Enzyme Inhibitors

The third core group of medicines used in treating patients with heart failure are vasodilators, or medicines that open up the arteries of the body to make the heart pumping function easier. I always tell patients that if you have a 1-horsepower motor pumping into a 1-inch tube or conduit, reducing the conduit to .5 inch is going to make the pump work even harder whereas increasing the conduit to 1.5 inches is going to make the pump work more efficiently. That has been the basic idea behind the use of a variety of medications called vasodilators, which includes angiotensin-converting enzyme inhibitors (ACEIs). When the body senses a decreased pumping action of the heart, it responds in a variety of ways to hold onto salt and water, but it also sends out chemical signals to narrow the arteries and veins of the body. This too is a homeostatic mechanism, with the goal of keeping the blood pressure stable, but in fact it represents one of the processes that serves to worsen or accelerate a patient's heart failure, as application of the aforementioned analogy of the pump and conduit makes clear.

You might be surprised to learn that it was less than a decade ago that a clinical trial showed that a combination of vasodilators (hydralazine and isosorbide dinitrate) results in a reduction in mortality rate for patients with heart failure. Since then, more and more information has become available about the ACEIs, a new class of agents that actually block the production of one of the substances that causes the blood vessels to go into spasm or constrict. This class of drugs has been shown to be one of the most effective treatments for heart failure not only in terms of reducing symptoms but also with respect to decreasing the mortality rate. In a clinical trial comparing the combination of hydralazine and isosorbide dinitrate with the ACEIs, the latter seem to have had a better effect on mortality rate. Drugs that fall within the ACEI category include captopril, enalapril, and lisinopril. There are still other drugs within this category that do not yet have specific approval for use in treating heart failure.

Despite the overwhelming evidence that these drugs are useful for treating patients with heart failure, it is estimated that perhaps only 25% to 40% of patients who should be on these drugs are actually taking them. There are some common side effects that can occur with the ACEIs that may cause the drugs to be discontinued in certain patients. Since these drugs open up the blood vessels, they can lower blood pressure, which may already be quite low in a patient with heart failure. They can also cause rashes and taste alteration (but these side effects are infrequent), as well as some worsening of the kidney function (but, again, this is infrequent and usually quickly reversible). On the other hand, they may improve kidney function in some patients and that is why it is so important to try these drugs in most patients. One of the most common reasons patients stop taking these drugs or physicians remain reluctant to prescribe them is that they can produce a cough. It has been estimated that the cough can occur in anywhere from 5% to 20% of patients, but my experience has been that much of the cough in patients with heart failure really is congestion or fluid in the lungs and that once the patient is adequately "dried out," the cough is no longer a problem. There are new drugs being investigated and developed that work in a fashion similar to the ACEIs but that will bypass some of the adverse effects, such as the cough. Also, as was the case earlier with digoxin, we do not know the ideal dose of an ACEI that a patient should be taking. Again, within the next few years we hope to have some better answers to our questions about these drugs.

The important point here is that these drugs have been shown to have such an important effect for heart failure patients that a serious attempt should be made to get most patients on these drugs while avoiding some of the side effects.

Summary

In this chapter we have talked about some of the basic approaches to treating heart failure, including fluid and salt restriction and the use of core medicines. There are still many other drugs and treatments that could be considered conventional. For example, if a patient cannot tolerate one of the ACEI drugs, substituting the combination of hydralazine and isosorbide dinitrate would be a reasonable alternative and would still be considered a good conventional approach. In other chapters we'll talk about some of the more advanced or investigational approaches to treating patients with heart failure. I want to emphasize, though, that unless a good foundation is established with conventional treatment, the more exotic investigational approaches are unlikely to succeed.

Chapter 8

Summary of Common Heart Failure Drugs
Indications, Doses, Side Effects, and Interactions with Other Drugs

It is clear that even for patients who are not yet symptomatic, there is a role for drug therapy in virtually everyone who has heart failure. In fact, most patients with heart failure end up taking at least two medications. As we find out more about how these medications work and what impact they have on survival and outcome, heart failure patients will probably, at least for the next decade, end up taking more and more medications. It is well known that with each new medication there is a risk of confusion regarding when it should be taken, what adverse side effects can be expected, and how it interacts with other drugs. (Appendix II lists resources for more information, including books that discuss in detail many of the side effects, indications, dosages, and so forth of each of the heart failure medications.)

I have long been aware of the cost of medications for heart failure patients. In fact, an inability to pay for some of the medications is not infrequently the reason a patient ends up back in the hospital with worsened heart failure. As I point out in a medical publication, the current average cost for just the core heart failure medications can easily approach over $1,000 each year. Although we are constantly reminded that the cost of drugs represents a small proportion of the cost of caring for patients with heart failure, it is unfortunately true that for most patients the percentage of the cost of medication paid for by the patient is far greater than the percentage of hospitalization or office visit charges the patient must assume as out-of-pocket expenses. Because of patients' concerns about the cost of medication, I am frequently asked if generic and brand name medications are equivalent. With few exceptions I generally recommend that generics be provided for most of my patients. There are, however, a couple of circumstances where the bioavailability or absorption is better with the brand name than with the generic drug. This should be discussed with your physician. Similarly, there can be wide range in the price of a medication, and I always encourage my patients to shop around, particularly for some of the more expensive medications. However, the pharmacy business has become quite competitive, and nowadays the large chains are often not significantly less expensive than your local pharmacist. I personally feel there is a very important role to be played by the local pharmacist, and I think many patients turn to that individual for a lot of advice regarding their health care. In fact, a recent survey found that Americans still rank the local pharmacist as the most honorable and ethical professional.

Finally, let me emphasize how important it is to always carry with you a current list of your medications, including their doses and how often you take them. This is critical whenever you visit a doctor, and if you are ever in an emergency situation, you will need to inform the emergency room doctor or nurse of your medications. I also recommend that patients enroll in the Medic Alert Program (1-800-736-3342); patients wear a bracelet or necklace that identifies their medical condition, treating doctor, and allergies or provides other critical medical information. At the end of this chapter I include a medication chart that I commonly use. I usually write the medications and dosing times in pencil so that they can be frequently updated. Many patients miniaturize this chart, and I have seen numerous variations that range from nothing more than a hand-scribbled note to a sophisticated computer printout by those patients so inclined. The important message here, however, is to always carry with you a current list of all your medications, including not only your prescription medications but also all the nonprescription medications (minerals, vitamins, aspirin, cold remedies, and so on) you might be taking.

Here are some general tips on taking medicines that I think are important and useful.

Tips on Taking Your Medicines

1. Know the name, dosage, actions, special instructions, and common side effects of all the medicines you are taking. Keep your medications handy. Bring them to all visits to your doctor's office.
2. Take your medicines as ordered. Even when you are feeling better, continue taking them on schedule. Never take more than has been prescribed, and do not stop taking them unless told to do so by your doctor.

3. It is preferable that you take your medicines at the same time each day to ensure a consistent level of the medicine in your bloodstream. If you have trouble figuring out a convenient schedule, ask for help. Sometimes following the chart shown at the end of this chapter is helpful.

4. Keep your medicines in their original container. Do not remove labels.

5. Ask your doctor before taking any over-the-counter medicines (including Dristan, Sudafed, Anacin, or any other cold pills or pain relievers, even aspirin).

6. Medicines can become outdated and therefore ineffective. If they are more than several months old, ask your pharmacist or doctor if they are still effective and safe.

7. Do not give your medicines to anyone, even if that person seems to have the same symptoms as you do.

8. It may take time for your body to adjust to a new medicine, and it may take time for the medicine to begin to work effectively. Sometimes you may have mild side effects during this period. Discuss them with your doctor. Sometimes another medicine can be prescribed. However, always report anything unusual when taking a new medication.

9. When a new medicine is prescribed, ask your pharmacist to give you only a 1-to-2-week supply until you are sure your body will tolerate it. (Your doctor may give you samples to see if you tolerate the new medication.) Call your doctor if you are running low on the samples to see if he or she wants you to continue with that medication.

10. Cost can be an important factor with medicines,

since most prescribed drugs can be expensive. However, you cannot afford *not* to take them. Discuss this with your doctor. Perhaps less expensive medicines can be substituted. Also, ask your doctor about available indigent programs, if you have such a need.

11. Many times there are helpful warnings and instructions on prescription bottles. For example, these may remind you to take the medication with food or after a meal. Generally, you should heed these instructions. However, patients sometimes run into problems with the warnings on bottles of potassium supplements, which advise taking these "with plenty of water." Since that is generally not the best advice for most heart failure patients, be sure to check with your doctor for more specific instructions.

12. If you miss a dose of a medication, check with your doctor rather than take an extra dose. Doses of certain heart failure medications too close together can often do more harm than good. Try *not* to miss doses.

Common Heart Failure Medications

In this section I list several of the drugs that are commonly used in treating patients with heart failure. I first list the generic name for the drug, as well as some of the common brand names for it. Then I provide some general information about the drug, list the common dose range and some of the common side effects. I then list some of the possible interactions.

Before I discuss each of the drug categories I am going

to tell you what one of my senior residents told me when I was an intern. He said, "Any drug can do anything." Basically, what he meant was that since most drugs can potentially produce a wide range of actions and side effects, you should take it seriously when a patient reports an unusual effect from a medication. I have always done so, even when the text books don't report a certain reaction. Everyone reacts differently to medications. Frankly, it is quite surprising to me how many people really do tolerate the many medications we use for treating heart failure.

As I mentioned earlier, there are many good books available that detail all of the effects, side effects, and dosages of drugs (some even show pictures of the medications), and these should be referred to. Almost everyone has access to a public library, which should contain one of the books that lists all the medications. For example, the *Physicians' Desk Reference* (*PDR*), which is updated every year, lists all the information available on over 3,000 drugs. You can look any drug up in this book, either by its generic name or its brand name, and read a brief description of it, including some of the clinical pharmacology about the drug as well as its indications and usages. The *PDR* also lists contraindications, or reasons you should not take the drug; warnings, particularly regarding the use of drugs during pregnancy; important precautions; and adverse reactions that may occur. Commonly, there is also a section on interactions with other drugs and specific information on what to do in the event of an overdose, as well as information regarding the specific dosage and administration—although many times the drugs that are used for heart failure are used in dosages that may differ from those listed for other indications, such as high blood pressure. Finally, the *PDR* will give you information about how the medication is supplied, that is, in what form and dosage. There is even a pictorial guide so that you can match up your pills with the picture to make sure you are taking the correct pill and the right dosage.

When your doctor prescribes a new medication, frequently he or she will give you a sample with a package insert that contains the same printed information that appears in the *PDR*. And when you go to a pharmacy to pick up a new prescription, you may want to ask the pharmacist to give you a copy of the package insert, which will detail all of this information. Many pharmacies nowadays are providing either computer printouts or standardized forms that describe a bit more about the medication the patient is taking, and because many pharmacies have all of a person's prescriptions on a computer, they can easily identify any potential interactions among the drugs that person is taking.

I think these are very positive moves, and I encourage most of my patients to refer to *PDR* or a similar kind of text to learn more about their medications. At the same time, however, I also warn them that if they read about any drug they'll be afraid to take it and that some faith has to be placed in their physician to prescribe the proper medication and the proper dosage to best treat their heart failure.

Just recently I was exploring the health section of one of the on-line computer services that are becoming so popular. A subscriber can look up a drug and read information on its indications, how to take the medication, what to do about missed doses and so on. However, I think it would be rather frightening for a patient to read all the side effects that were listed without having a physician, nurse, or pharmacist there to add a comment or two about how often these side effects actually occur in their experience. I believe more and more people will probably get their drug information in this way as we expand our "communication superhighways," and I hope this process does not have a negative effect on doctor–patient relationships or on a patient's compliance with medications.

Digoxin

The common brand name for digoxin is Lanoxin.

General Information. Digoxin is a medication that is commonly used to help the heart beat stronger and somewhat slower and more regularly. It is commonly used to control irregular heart rhythms, such as atrial fibrillation, but has also been shown to improve the heart's pumping function. Digitalis, an older preparation of this drug made directly from the foxglove plant, is rarely used today.

Common Dosages. Digoxin is used in a variety of dosages, ranging from 0.125 milligrams to 0.375 milligrams daily, and is usually taken as a single dose. However, digoxin is one of those medications for which the dosage is greatly dependent on many other conditions, such as age, kidney function, and other medications you are taking. Therefore, the dosage has to be adjusted very carefully by your doctor and may even change as you take other medicines. Some patients may only take doses several times a week, rather than daily.

Common Side Effects. Digoxin is a medication that actually can have a fairly high incidence of side effects, primarily because of all the drug interactions and conditions that alter the level of digoxin in a patient's blood. Up to 30% of all hospitalized patients taking digoxin have some degree of toxicity from it. Most of the side effects, however, usually indicate that the patient has too much digoxin in his or her system. This is called digoxin toxicity. Loss of appetite and nausea can be very early side effects indicating that there is too much digoxin in the blood. A patient may also have blurred vision or see a yellow halo around objects and lights and may have serious, as well as nonserious, irregular heartbeats and excessive slowing of the pulse. Occasionally, digoxin causes some increase in and tenderness of the breast tissue in both men and women. The dosage of digoxin needs to be carefully monitored and adjusted in anyone who has an impairment in kidney function, a common condition in patients who have heart failure and in elderly patients. Impaired condition function can lead to increased digoxin in the blood.

Drug Interactions. When taking digoxin patients need an adequate amount of potassium and magnesium in their blood. Many drugs can raise the level of digoxin in the blood, including quinidine, verapamil and amiodarone (Cordarone). Also, certain antibiotics, such as erythromycin, may increase the absorption of digoxin. Even certain foods can interact with the absorption of this medication; eating oat bran at the same time you take your digoxin dose can alter absorption and give you a lower level of digoxin in the blood than expected. Certain antacids, on the other hand, can also lower the absorption.

Most problems with digoxin occur when there is too much of it in the blood. The following conditions can predispose a person to digoxin toxicity:

1. Kidney failure
2. Too little potassium, too little magnesium, or too much calcium

3. Severe heart disease (New York Heart Association Class III or IV)
4. A recent heart attack
5. Advanced age
6. Thyroid disease, especially hypothyroidism (underactive thyroid)
7. Hypoxic states (not enough oxygen)
8. Multiple drug therapy (especially including quinidine or amiodarone)
9. Other heart problems, including preexisting electrical abnormalities of the heart (A-V [Atrioventricular] block)

Diuretics (Water Pills)

Diuretics are a general class of medications that help the body rid itself of extra fluid. There are various types of water pills that act on different portions of the kidney. The majority of patients end up taking one of what we call the "loop" diuretics, such as furosemide. (The loop is a special part of the kidney.) Table 8.1 lists some common diuretics, along with their brand names and usual dosages.

TABLE 8.1. Common Diuretics

Common brand name	Generic name	Usual dosage
Aldactone	Spironolactone	25–100 mg/day
Bumex	Bumetanide	0.5–20 mg/day
Diuril	Chlorothiazide	50–100 mg/day
Dyrenium	Triamterene	100–300 mg/day
Edecrin	Ethacrynic acid	50–200 mg/day
Hygroton	Chlorthalidone	25–100 mg/day
Lasix	Furosemide	20–400 mg/day
Midamor	Amiloride	5–10 mg/day
Zaroxolyn	Metolazone	2.5–10 mg/day

General Information.   Through a variety of different actions in the kidney, diuretics help to rid the body of excess fluid. Some diuretics, such as spironolactone, triamterene, and amiloride, help retain potassium in the bloodstream whereas others tend to cause loss of potassium in the urine. Because these drugs help get rid of fluid, they can cause light-headedness, fatigue, thirst, diarrhea, or constipation. Usually, the side effects are caused by the alteration of levels of electrolytes or other chemicals within the body. For example, by lowering the potassium level too much diuretics can precipitate irregular heartbeats, weakness, and even cardiac arrest. They also occasionally cause skin rashes and hives. Another possible side effect is an increase in the uric acid level, which can precipitate an episode of gout. The thiazides (chlorothiazide, chlorthalidone, hydrochlorothiazide) can alter the cholesterol level, and furosemide and ethacrynic acid can cause hearing damage.

Interactions.   Many diuretics contain sulfa, and a person with a sulfa allergy can be highly sensitive to these drugs (ethacrynic acid, however, does *not* contain sulfa). Diuretics can also interact with a wide variety of the so-called nonsteroidal anti-inflammatory drugs, such as Indocin or Motrin (ibuprofen). They can also cause sensitivity to sunlight (this may be particularly true of triamterene).

Because these medications cause an increase in urination, patients may find that there is more frequent urination, particularly at night, and should therefore avoid taking a dose of a diuretic immediately before going to bed at night.

Angiotensin-Converting Enzyme Inhibitors (ACEIs)

There is a wide variety of ACEIs currently available. Commonly used ACEIs include captopril (brand name,

Capoten); enalapril (Vasotec); and lisinopril (Prinivil, Zestril). The doses of these drugs vary a great deal depending on the patient's ability to tolerate the drug and on underlying conditions, such as renal function and age. There seems to be wide variation among physicians not only in terms of the dose they prescribe but often in the regimen they suggest for taking these medications. There is still a question regarding whether higher or lower doses of the ACEIs are needed to treat heart failure adequately, and a clinical trial is currently under way to help answer that question. Therefore, with a drug like Capoten, for example, you will often find some patients taking as little as 6.25 milligrams twice a day whereas others may take up to 75 milligrams four times a day; generally, I like my patients to take Capoten at least three or four times a day in the highest dose they can tolerate. The typical dosage with Vasotec ranges anywhere from 2.5 milligrams once a day to 10 milligrams twice a day; I generally recommend twice daily dosing in the largest dose tolerated. For example, the dosage used in several of the studies showing the effectiveness of Vasotec was 10 milligrams twice a day. When these drugs are used to treat high blood pressure, Capoten twice daily or Vasotec once daily is adequate, but for heart failure more frequent doses are required. The usual dosage for lisinopril (Prinivil, Zestril) is 5 to 20 milligrams once a day.

General Information. ACEIs help open up the arteries of the body and are commonly used to treat high blood pressure and heart failure. We are discovering that these drugs actually do many other important things in the body. It is generally best to take these drugs on an empty stomach, before eating.

Common Side Effects. The most common side effects of ACEIs are cough, loss of taste, a drop in the blood pressure, and, occasionally, worsening of kidney function. These drugs can also cause sore throat, fever, skin rash, and what is known as *angioedema*, a condition in which a person's throat swells up causing difficulty in breathing. On rare occasions they can also lower the white cell count, which makes fighting off infections more difficult. Since patients who are on diuretics may have more episodes of low blood pressure, sometimes the diuretics are reduced a bit prior to starting an ACEI. Also, these drugs can help retain potassium in the bloodstream and therefore have to be used with caution in people who are already on potassium supplementation or in those who are taking a diuretic that may retain additional potassium. Occasionally, some of the anti-inflammatory drugs, even aspirin, can increase the potential of an ACEI to worsen kidney function, and recently it has been suggested that aspirin may in fact negate some of the effect of an ACEI. It has also been found that patients taking lithium can have a much higher level of lithium in the blood when taking one of the ACEIs.

Nitroglycerin

There are many ways in which nitroglycerin can be introduced into the bloodstream. There are pills that are either placed under the tongue or swallowed, as well as patches and creams that are absorbed through the skin. See Table 8.2 for the common brand name and usual dosages.

General Information.   Nitroglycerin is used to help dilate the veins and arteries and to improve blood flow to the heart; it may also improve blood flow through the lungs.

TABLE 8.2. Nitroglycerin

Common brand name	Generic name	Usual dosage
Imdur	Isosorbide mononitrate	30–120 mg once/day
Ismo	Isosorbide mononitrate	10–40 mg twice/day
Isordil tablets or capsules	Isosorbide dinitrate	10–40 mg 3 or 4 times/day
Nitro-Dur and Transderm-Nitro	Nitroglycerin patches	0.2–0.6 mg/hour

Common Dosages. The dosages and administration patterns vary so much with the various nitroglycerin medications that you should consult your physician for further information. In general, these drugs are underdosed, in my opinion, because of concern about low blood pressure.

Common Side Effects. Common side effects with nitroglycerin include flushing of the face and neck and headache, which occur usually shortly after taking the medication. Nitroglycerin can also cause skin rashes, fast heart rate, and dizziness or light-headedness, especially when the patient gets up from a seated position. Frequently, the headaches can be minimized by taking Tylenol prior to taking the medication.

Nitroglycerin patches can cause irritation to the skin, which can be minimized by rotating the patch from site to site. Doctors used to recommend that the patches be worn an entire day at a time, but doctors now commonly suggest that they be removed for at least 8 hours during the day to maximize their effectiveness and avoid what is called nitrate tolerance. This is especially true in patients using these drugs to treat *angina pectoris* (chest pain).

Interactions. Because nitroglycerin can lower blood pressure and open up the arteries, it certainly can worsen or accentuate the feeling of light-headedness that is produced by other medicines that also lower blood pressure, such as diuretics, ACEIs, and other vasodilators.

Other Vasodilators

There are other drugs besides the ACEIs—for example, hydralazine (a common brand name is Apresoline)—that open up the arteries. In fact, some of them have been used for longer than the ACEIs. I am going to mention two classes of these drugs—direct vasodilators, such as hydralazine, and calcium channel blockers, such as diltiazem or nifedipine—because they are still commonly used for people who cannot tolerate the ACEIs; sometimes they are even used in addition to the ACEIs.

General Information. Vasodilators act directly on the arteries to increase their diameter and thereby decrease the resistance that the failing heart has to pump against. In fact, it was the combination of this medication (hydralazine) and isosorbide dinitrate that was one of the first combinations shown to lower the mortality rate of patients who had heart failure.

Common Dosages. The usual dosage of hydralazine is 10 to 75 milligrams three to four times a day, but, as is true of so many other medicines we have discussed, there is a wide range of dosing and frequency in the clinical use of this drug. It is my practice to generally maximize the dose and have patients take this drug four times a day. That was the regimen used in the trial that showed hydralazine to be so successful; until there is evidence otherwise, I generally try to duplicate the doses of drugs that were shown in studies to be useful. There are, however, many clinical situations where lower doses of hydralazine are in fact used.

Common Side Effects. As you would expect with any drug that opens up the arteries, headache and low blood pressure—perhaps even a sudden drop in blood pressure—can occur. Hydralazine has some particular side effects, including a drug-related fever, skin rash, and, very frequently, a laboratory abnormality called a "positive ANA," which can indicate a lupus-like syndrome. (Systemic lupus erythematosus is a disease that can cause joint pain, skin rashes, and damage to the kidneys and many other organs.) Hydralazine can also cause headache, loss of appetite, nausea and vomiting, diarrhea, and even an increased amount of chest pain in some patients.

Drug Interactions. Hydralazine may interact with any other drug that has some effect on blood pressure, and this drug should be used with extreme caution in patients receiving certain forms of antidepressants. When hydralazine is taken with food there are higher levels of the drug in the blood; therefore, lower doses may be used.

Calcium Channel Blockers

Since calcium channel blockers also cause opening up of the arteries and veins, they are anticipated to have some use in treating heart failure. However, some of the older forms of these drugs also have the effect of making the heart muscle weaker and, therefore, are really of limited use in treating patients with heart failure. There are new calcium channel blockers that are being developed; in fact,

TABLE 8.3. Common Calcium Channel Blockers

Common brand name	Generic name	Usual dosage
Calan	Verapamil	120–360 mg/day
Cardene	Nicardipine	60–120 mg/day
Cardizem or Dilacor XR	Diltiazem	90–240 mg/day
Norvasc	Amlodipine	5–20 mg/day
Plendil	Felodipine	5–10 mg/day
Procardia	Nifedipine	30–60 mg/day

clinical trials with at least a couple of them are now being conducted specifically in patients who have heart failure.

Table 8.3 lists a few of the many calcium channel blockers. Although the jury is still out on the general usefulness of these drugs in treating heart failure, there are certain forms of heart failure, such as hypertrophic cardiomyopathy, for which these drugs are the mainstay of therapy. I suggest that you discuss these drugs with your doctor to see if they are useful for your particular form of heart failure.

As would be expected, hypotension is a common adverse effect with this group of drugs. They also can produce a rapid heartbeat and a sensation of palpitations along with flushing; headaches; and, commonly, leg edema that is not related to the degree of heart failure. Since they can also alter the electrical system of the heart to varying degrees and cause heart block (impaired electrical conduction between the upper and lower chambers of the heart), these drugs have to be used carefully with other drugs that have this effect, such as beta blockers or digoxin.

Constipation, exacerbated by other heart failure medications and by the fluid restriction imposed on heart failure patients, is a common side effect with many calcium channel blockers and is the reason often cited by patients for drug intolerance.

Coumadin

Another drug commonly used in patients with heart failure is the medication known as warfarin sodium, commonly known by the brand name Coumadin. This drug is a potent medication that works as an anticoagulant, or blood thinner. Drugs of this type are used in patients with heart failure either to prevent the formation of blood clots in the heart or to prevent the *embolization,* or breaking loose, of blood clots that may already be present in the heart. When a person has atrial fibrillation, the upper chambers of the heart are not beating on a regular basis, a condition that can result in *blood stasis,* or slowing of the current of circulating blood. Blood that is not being ejected from the upper chambers in a normal fashion can tend to clot, or coagulate, there. When a *thrombus,* or blood clot, forms, there is the risk that a microscopic portion of it might break off, go elsewhere in the body—to the brain, kidney, lung, even the intestine—and cause serious medical problems.

Blood clotting is also a problem when the heart muscle is weak—generally, with an ejection fraction of less than 25%, blood clots can form within the left ventricle. And since blood clots frequently form inside the heart muscle after large heart attacks, anticoagulants are used to prevent additional clots from forming and to allow the body to put a thin coating of tissue around the existing blood clots so that embolization is prevented.

Regardless of the reason for their using a blood thinner, patients need to be aware that this medicine works by blocking the synthesis of some of the factors that normally allow the blood to clot. Most of these are factors dependent on Vitamin K, and, in fact, changes in the diet to either increase or decrease the intake of foods rich in Vitamin K can significantly alter the effectiveness of the blood thinner. Therefore, the patient should try to keep his or her intake of foods rich in Vitamin K constant, if at all possible, when taking Coumadin. There are also various medications that interact with Coumadin to make it either more or less effective; such medications therefore expose the patient either to bleeding, if the anticoagulation capability becomes too extreme, or to additional risk of blood clotting. A great many substances can increase the activity of Coumadin and therefore increase the risk of bleeding, including alcohol, allopurinol, aspirin, amiodarone (Cordarone), many antibiotics, some diuretics, ibuprofen (Motrin), indomethacin (Indocin), naproxen (Naprosyn), quinidine, and thyroid medications. Medications that can decrease the activity of Coumadin and therefore increase the risk of blood clotting include antacids, antihistamines, many sleeping pills, oral contraceptives, and Vitamin C.

Because of the narrow range of clotting ability in which the blood must be maintained, patients taking Coumadin are asked to have their blood checked frequently to make sure that it is clotting to the right degree. This is determined by measuring prothrombin time, better known as "pro time" or PT. Prothrombin is converted to thrombin in the body, which helps form blood clots. This simple test can be done at any laboratory by sampling blood either from a vein or from a finger prick. The pro time may be reported as the number of seconds it takes for the blood to clot compared to a normal control; it is now more commonly being reported as an International Normalized Ratio, or INR.

Coumadin therapy can be very important for patients with heart failure, damaged heart valves, or irregular heartbeats, but close follow-up by the physician and frequent checks on adequate anticoagulation are necessary. This certainly is one situation where patients should discuss any planned surgery—no matter how minor—with the doctor who manages their heart failure, and there must always be a single doctor in charge of management of Coumadin therapy. Patients taking Coumadin should also discuss with that doctor any additional medication another doctor may prescribe, including any over-the-counter medication.

Potassium Supplements

Potassium supplements are often prescribed for patients taking diuretics. As I mentioned earlier, when increased urine is passed through the kidney, potassium, along with other electrolytes, is frequently excreted in increased amounts as well. On the basis of an analysis of the potassium level in your blood, and a consideration of the other medications you might be taking that may have any effect on either retaining or losing potassium, your doctor may recommend that you take a potassium supplement. A normal amount of potassium is critical for the day-to-day functioning of your body. There are an enormous number of potassium products available on the market, and your physician will try to find a product that will work for you and that is most convenient for you. These products come in tablet, liquid, and powder form, and most patients have their preference. Many patients with heart failure end up taking extremely large doses of potassium because of the large doses of diuretics they are on; to reduce the number of potassium pills or the amount of liquid a patient must consume, a physician might decide at some point to pre-scribe an additional medicine that helps retain potassium. These specifics should be discussed directly with your doctor. There are also problems that can develop with too much potassium; these typically occur in patients who have kidney malfunction or are taking drugs that help retain potassium, such as spironolactone or even the angiotensin-converting enzyme inhibitors (ACEIs), such as captopril or enalapril. Potassium can be irritating to the stomach and intestinal tract. Generally, heart failure pa-tients take these medications at meals with some fluid, although, because of the fluid restriction most of these patients are on, not as much fluid as pharmacists usually recommend.

Lately I have been asked about patients' taking po-tassium supplements that are available at health food stores. While the potassium salt is acceptable, the problem is that most of these over-the-counter preparations have very low concentrations. The average heart failure patient takes 20 milliequivalents of potassium twice a day, the equivalent of 1,500 milligrams of potassium twice a day, and most prescription potassium tablets or liquids come in doses between 600 to 1,500 milligrams per tablet or spoon-ful. The common health food store preparations I have seen contain somewhere between 50 and 90 milligrams, so a patient would end up taking many of these potassium pills to get the same effect. Unless you have discussed this with your doctor and it has been determined that the po-tassium supplement you find in the health food store can adequately replace your potassium losses, this would not be a wise thing to gamble with.

One of the common effects of a low potassium level is the muscle cramps that generally occur in the legs, feet, or even the hands. It is important to know that a variety of other electrolyte imbalances, such as low calcium, low magnesium, or low sodium, can also cause these cramps, as can certain medications, including nifedipine (Procardia), terbutaline (Brethine), cimetidine (Tagamet), and lithium. Actually, in most cases the cause is usually not found. Leg cramps that occur at night are particularly disturbing; they may awaken the person from sleep and may last from several minutes to several hours. They occur more frequently as a person ages, and it has been estimated that up to 70% of people over the age of 50 have some form of nocturnal leg cramps. However, for patients with heart failure who are taking large doses of diuretics and potassium, I always think it is worthwhile to check the potassium level when the patient reports such cramps. When the cramps continue despite normal levels of electrolytes, then other avenues can be pursued. Doctors commonly prescribe quinine pills; I often suggest that patients take small sips of quinine water, or tonic water. A recent study comparing quinine to Vitamin E showed that quinine was the only effective treatment. There are other drugs available, but often some simple exercises that a doctor can recommend may be all that's needed for most cases of leg cramps. The important point here is that since muscle cramps may be a sign that potassium is low, you should be alert to them and should report any occurrence to your doctor.

Patient: _____

Medications	6 AM	7 AM	8 AM	9 AM	10 AM	11 AM	12 NN	1 PM	2 PM	3 PM	4 PM	5 PM	6 PM	7 PM	8 PM	9 PM	10 PM	11 PM	12 MD	1 AM	2 AM	3 AM	4 AM	5 AM

FIGURE 8.1. Heart failure medication schedule.

Chapter 9

Heart Transplantation

To be able to talk about heart transplantation as an every-day event when not so long ago this phenomenon was considered to be in the realm of science fiction is truly remarkable. However, after years and years of research and hard work, primarily by the pioneers of heart transplantation at Stanford University, heart transplants are in fact an everyday occurrence here in the United States and worldwide. From my years of serving as a heart transplant cardiologist I have great respect for this procedure that can transform a critically ill heart failure patient into someone who has enormous vigor and stamina. However, there remain many caveats for most patients with heart failure, and I want to review some of these briefly.

The first thing to consider are the numbers, which play an important role in understanding how transplantation fits into the treatment picture for heart failure. Despite the major advances that have been made in heart transplantation, the cold hard fact is that there are a limited number of donor organs. There are many reasons for this, but it seems that we have reached a plateau, with approximately 3,000 heart transplants being done annually worldwide and probably about 2,000 of those being done in the United States. In fact, according to the most recent official report of the Registry of the International Society for Heart and Lung Transplantation, the total number of transplants performed worldwide dipped well below 3,000 in the year 1992, to only 2,709. What that means, in effect, is that the availability of donor organs is far less than the need for them. Many attempts have been made to educate the public in general about the desperate need for donor organs, but there has been little success. Unfortunately, there is a great deal of mythologizing about heart transplantation, and this has kept families from allowing their loved ones to become organ donors. The tabloid stories of organs sold on a "black market" do nothing but inhibit much-needed organ donation. Nonetheless, even if we were to double or triple or even quadruple the number of organ donors, that would barely touch the problem for the millions of patients who have advanced heart failure.

The major question then is, Who should be selected to receive a heart transplant? The criteria have certainly changed since heart transplantation first began in the early 1960s and have even changed within the past decade. By and large, the person who needs a heart transplant is someone who has end-stage heart disease that is no longer amenable to medical or other surgical treatments. Obviously, however, since the wait can be quite long for a donor organ, we no longer want to select patients who are so far advanced that their survival is measured in days, weeks, or even months. Because of the high demand for donor organs, people may wait for a heart transplant for many months or even well beyond a year without getting the call to receive their new heart. That leaves it up to the referring doctor to decide when the patient should be referred. I generally encourage referrals to heart transplant centers sooner rather than later. If the referral is made at too late a stage in the disease process, the patient often will not survive to get the heart transplant. When the referral is made early, the patient benefits because frequently the staff at a heart transplant center is also experienced in caring for heart failure patients and can look at other options besides transplantation or use other treatments while the patient waits for the transplant.

Besides a severely damaged heart, there are other criteria that determine who can become a heart transplant recipient. A person should have no other organs that are failing. In other words, while the heart may be severely affected, a good candidate for transplantation has kidneys, lungs, liver, and so on, in good working order, thus allowing for a good recovery after the heart transplant and limiting future complications. Additionally, there should not be any serious psychological or social problems, since the burden of waiting for and then receiving a new heart, along with the psychological effects of the immunosuppressive medication, can worsen any existing psychological problem the patient may have. Conditions such as drug and/or alcohol abuse, an unstable family situation, or a family lacking strong supports are frequently reasons to exclude someone as a possible heart transplant recipient. Another complicating problem can be a serious illness that affects the body as a whole, such as lupus erythematosus or insulin-requiring diabetes.

The question of age is a common one: Who is too old to receive a heart transplant? One of the interesting things that we have learned over the past decade is that the older patients do not do any worse than younger patients when it comes to receiving a heart transplant. In fact, there is some evidence that suggests that the older person with the more quiescent immune system fares even better than the younger patient. Therefore, it is not unusual to see patients even well into their sixties being considered for heart transplantation.

So, to summarize, the ideal heart transplantation candidate is someone who has very advanced heart failure with a reasonable 1-year life expectancy, who does not have any other major illness or any other organ that is severely affected, and who has a strong psychological and social support system. However, because of the very limited number of donor organs available, the candidate must often be one who has tried and failed other conventional and even experimental treatment programs.

With that in mind, let us consider what might be involved should a patient require a heart transplant evaluation. Unfortunately, one of the primary considerations is the form of insurance a patient has. Not all insurance policies will cover transplant services and patients often discover these limitations too late. Usually, when a doctor refers a patient to a heart transplant center, the center will screen the patient's insurance coverage prior to beginning any further evaluation. After the first hurdle is cleared in terms of assuring insurance coverage or clarifying the financial arrangements, there is usually an extensive review of the testing that has already been performed as a preliminary screen to make sure that the person is indeed a reasonable candidate. Then the patient is commonly admitted to the heart transplant center for a short evaluation, which often includes repeating some of the tests that were done in the past, such as an echocardiogram, a MUGA test, and blood tests. Frequently, the patient and the family meet with a social worker and/or a psychologist or psychiatrist to determine the extent of support that will be available and the potential for psychological problems. Actually, I think most patients find this part of the evaluation a relief, for it helps to bring to the forefront some of those anxieties that are present in anyone who has suffered from heart failure for many years.

Since patients often have to wait so long for a heart to become available, as I mentioned earlier, the process of actually trying to pick the optimal timing for a heart transplant and to decide which patients can wait longer for a transplant and which cannot is a critical part of the transplant evaluation. Earlier I talked about the cardiopulmonary exercise test and the important information it gives us in evaluating patients with heart failure and in predicting long-term survival (see Chapter 3). Heart transplant centers use this technique to help them decide who needs a heart transplant and when. Recent studies have shown that patients who do well on the cardiopulmonary exercise test can be reasonably managed on medical treatments alone and may in fact not need a heart transplant. On the other hand, a very poor performance would suggest the need for heart transplantation earlier rather than later.

One of the tests that is frequently repeated at a heart transplant center is the placement of a Swan-Ganz catheter to measure the pressures within the heart and lungs; this test not only looks at what the absolute pressures are but is also capable of assessing the degree to which the high pressures in the lungs and heart can be reversed. This, of course, is a critically important determination to make; if a patient has very high pressures in the lungs that cannot be reversed simply by putting in a new heart or pump, the new heart will be damaged by the high pressures almost immediately. Recognizing this fact was instrumental in helping us overcome some of the early disasters in heart transplantation. There are a variety of medicines that can be used to test whether the pressures in a patient's lungs can be lowered and to predict how the patient might do after the damaged heart is replaced with a new one. If the pressures in the lungs cannot be suitably lowered, the transplant doctors begin to think of alternative strategies for the patient, including implanting a donor heart that is larger than normal or even transplanting both a new heart and lungs. Occasionally it may mean declaring the patient to be unsuitable for transplantation.

At the end of the transplant evaluation a judgment is made as to whether the patient is a candidate for a transplant at that time or whether judgment will be deferred. If the patient does become a transplant candidate and is put on an active waiting list, a period of great stress and emotional turmoil then begins. As one of my patients told me years ago, "This is really an awkward feeling, because you are waiting to live while you are waiting for another person to die." Such thoughts and feelings, as well as the constraints imposed on the patient's lifestyle by the heart failure, make this a very stressful time for patient and family alike.

I think it is important to say a few words about organ donors. As you would expect, organ donors are usually young people who have suffered some kind of injury and cannot be kept alive without artificial means but whose organs are undamaged. Typically, this is a young person who has been in a motor vehicle accident and has suffered brain death but whose other organs are functioning normally. Frequently, multiple organs, including kidneys, liver, heart, and lungs, are donated. A great deal of effort has gone into educating medical centers in this country on how to identify and take care of a potential organ donor so that those organs that can be used for life in another patient and patients are salvaged and preserved.

Because of the short supply of organs for transplantation, some of the early stringent criteria applied to organ donors are now obsolete. I remember when we would automatically turn down a potential heart donor over the age of 35. Now, with the ability to assess a donor's heart function with echos and with angiograms to look at the arteries to make sure they are normal, older organ donors are being carefully considered. Although I said earlier that the number of organ donors could never keep pace with the number of potential recipients, I think we should nevertheless continue to increase awareness of the need for organ donors. I have seen the families of many patients become interested in being organ donors themselves and place organ donation stickers on their driver's license during the period of time when their loved one was waiting for a heart transplant. I think the decision to become an organ donor is best done with forethought, and I believe the topic of organ donation should be discussed among families, with members' making their wishes known, at a time when the family is not in crisis. I do not think I can recall a single instance where an organ donor's family regretted having donated organs to the needy individual.

Other questions often asked about heart transplantation involve some of the hard data, including the overall survival statistics and what life is like after a heart transplant. I think many of these issues are best discussed with the staff of individual transplant centers, but I'd like to give just some brief outlines to clear up any of the myths surrounding heart transplantation. The overall 1-year survival rate for patients undergoing routine heart transplantation is currently somewhere between 80% and 90%. Even 5 years after transplantation more than 70% of the patients remain alive. This is a remarkable contrast to the survival statistics gathered when heart transplantation was in its infancy in the early 1960s. Various factors are responsible for this marked improvement, especially (1) our ability to biopsy the heart and look for rejection and (2) the development of better immunosuppressive drugs, particularly cyclosporine. It was really the introduction of this drug that made heart transplantation a procedure that could be done in many medical centers rather than in just a few specialized ones. Another major advance has been the development of sophisticated heart transplant teams who are aware of all the problems a patient may have in both the pre- and the posttransplant period.

A heart biopsy remains the best way to look for evidence of rejection of the heart. Biopsies are usually done frequently within the first several months after transplantation and are continued at less frequent intervals, if the patient's condition warrants, for the entire life of the patient. There is also frequent monitoring of the immunosuppressive drug levels, and transplant cardiologists are always on the lookout for the development of a special kind of rejection that causes blocking of the arteries, which could lead to a heart attack or even sudden death. As you may know, the new heart is placed into the chest cavity without any nerves attached to the patient; therefore, any difficulty the heart may have may go undetected because of the person's inability to feel pain. The patient with a heart transplant lives a scrutinized life, but virtually none of the transplant patients I know would trade this life for their former one of advanced heart failure.

There are various other problems that go with heart transplantation, including high blood pressure, excess hair growth, elevation of the blood lipids, and the omnipresent risk of serious infection. Nonetheless, I think patients feel that the heart transplant was their last chance for survival, and the majority of patients enjoy a great deal of symptomatic relief. I think everyone has seen a picture of the heart transplant softball teams or picnics that take place throughout this country. It is certainly rewarding to see very sick people transformed into healthy ones. We can only be hopeful that further advances not only in transplanting donor hearts but in finding better, safer ways for detecting rejection of the heart and for immunosuppressing the patient will be made in the decades ahead.

Many of the heart transplant programs have strong support groups not only for patients who have already had their transplant but for those who are waiting for a transplant. Perhaps a support group is a good place for the heart failure patient considering transplantation to start; the group can give such an individual a patient's perspective on the pleasures and problems of heart transplantation.

Chapter 10

Experimental Approaches for Treating Heart Failure

What Clinical Trials Are All About

With almost every patient I see with heart failure I end up discussing some of the experimental approaches for treatment at some point. I don't always do it at the first visit because, let's face it, the terms *experimental* and *investigational* conjure up the concept of a mad doctor in his lab doing work on guinea pigs. Because at some point you may be asked to consider some of these experimental approaches, I want to give you some of my very strong opinions about what an experimental approach really is and how you should consider it.

First of all, you should remember that many of the drugs we are now using as conventional therapy went through periods of testing when they, in fact, were the new investigational drug. Take the example of the angiotensin-converting enzyme inhibitors (ACEIs), such as captopril or enalapril, which are now part of the core conventional treatment we use in so many patients with heart failure. It was only about a decade ago that these drugs were experimental. I remember quite clearly during my residency training admitting patients to the hospital who were going to receive the drug captopril as an experimental agent. We took many precautions: we measured patients' blood pressure, ran blood chemistries and urine analyses, and examined patients closely each day, checking them in the sitting and the standing position. Now these drugs require a minimum of follow-up testing and are given out routinely by doctors all across the country. The ease with which we now use these drugs is the result of the many hours and long years of hard work that physicians and scientists devoted to their development. However, it is also due in great part to the many thousands of patients who participated in clinical trials using these drugs. I think those patients would agree that they benefited from a drug, established decades later as quite useful, much sooner than would otherwise have been possible.

When I have patients who are reluctant to participate in a clinical trial because they fear they are going to be treated as a guinea pig or have concerns about the effect of the drug, I (or one of my experienced nurses) usually tell them that, in my opinion, patients who enter clinical trials get even better care than those who do not. Not only do they get the frequent examinations and tests that are mandated by the treatment protocol, but the amount of caring and checking up they receive usually goes way beyond what is required by the sponsoring agency. There is always some complaint in the United States about a drug not being released at a fast enough rate or not being available here although it is available in Europe, but I think, on the whole, that Americans are fortunate to have fair and compassionate rules regulating the development, testing, and introduction of new drugs.

If you are invited to participate in a clinical trial, you may want to ask some of the following key questions when discussing the investigational treatment with a physician or nurse. (You should know that before any human trials begin there will have been extensive animal testing to delineate dosing and side effects.) First of all, you should know whether the study you are asked to participate in is a Phase II, a Phase III, or even a Phase IV trial. The differences have to do with the stage of development the drug is in, the number of people who have been exposed to it, and the questions that are being asked. Usually, Phase II trials involve the early development of the drug in human beings; they may, for example, be conducted to determine what the proper dosage should be. These trials are usually small, very well controlled, and of short duration.

A Phase III trial is usually broader, and the dosage has been well defined. The sponsoring agency is looking at the overall effectiveness of the drug as well as at any side effects that may not have been apparent in the past. It may also be looking at the overall efficacy and safety of the drug over a longer period of time.

A phase IV trial involves a drug that is already on the market. The sponsor may now be looking at such issues as the efficacy of using the drug once a day rather than in a multiple-dose regimen or may be comparing the drug to another one that is also already on the market. With Phase II and Phase III drug trials patients get the added benefit of receiving a drug long before it is approved. The Phase IV drug trial only asks patients to help answer a question about an already approved drug; there is no benefit in terms of getting a truly experimental agent earlier than would otherwise be possible.

You should be aware that many drug trials are placebo

controlled, which means that a certain percentage of the patients in a trial, frequently half, will get a *placebo*, or inert substance, and not the new drug in question. This is one of the main ways to determine if a new drug does what it is supposed to do. If, for example, the patients who got Drug X get much better whereas those who got the placebo get much worse, then it is clear that Drug X is a good drug. However, the opposite can be true: there can be negative effects in the patients who got the drug as compared to those who got the placebo. These negative effects can be poor tolerance of the drug, or even increased mortality. Commonly, in addition to being placebo controlled, drug trials are "double blind," which means that neither patients nor their doctors know who is getting the real drug and who is getting the placebo. There can also be a crossover; that is, for a period of time the patient gets the real drug and then later crosses over to a period of placebo, or vice versa. Again, usually neither the patient nor the doctor knows which substance, the drug or the placebo, is being given. A *randomized* study means that the sponsoring agency will determine which patients receive which substance and in what order; this is done to avoid any bias the doctor may have toward giving the real drug to the sicker patients and the placebo to the healthier ones.

Heart failure drug trials are usually looking for one of several effects or for a combination of effects. An effect can be an increase in survival rate, an increase in exercise tolerance, or, better yet, an improvement in the cardiopulmonary exercise test result, or peak oxygen consumption. An effect can also be a decrease in the number of extra heartbeats, an improvement in the ejection fraction, or an overall improvement or amelioration of symptoms. Surprisingly, it has been only recently that questionnaires have been developed to measure a patient's quality of life and that improvement in quality of life has been considered an important end point in a clinical trial.

Once a clinical trial is mentioned to you, you will usually be given written as well as other information regarding the purpose of the trial, its objectives, your exact risks and benefits, and your level of participation. You should study the written material carefully, but remember that you can pose any questions you may have directly to your doctors and nurses, who are the investigators for the trial. Doctors try to match their objectives and commitments for investigating a drug with their responsibilities in meeting their patients' needs. For example, I will try to get those patients who I think are on rather tenuous ground and with whom I'd like to try a new treatment into a treatment trial that is a Phase II or even a Phase III clinical trial of short duration so that they are not committed to a trial that may go on for 2 or 3 years. That does not mean that if there should be a problem or a patient needs other treatment, he or she cannot get out of the trial; almost all trials have some fail-safe mechanism so that the patient can exit the trial at any point. A good match should be attempted between a patient's clinical needs and the nature of the available trials.

Another issue that should not be overlooked is that in many clinical trials there is financial support for much, if not all, of the testing to be done; often, patients are unlikely to incur any charge. Again, the physician investigator should try to match the patient's needs with the requirements of the trial. For example, for most patients it is important to have a recent measurement of the pressures within the heart and lungs. This usually requires a brief hospital admission, but, as we all know, even a brief hospital admission can be expensive with today's hospital costs. Therefore, I will frequently match patients who are in need of such a measurement with an ongoing trial that will allow them to come into the hospital and get such a measurement without charge. Usually, as part of the trial, the measurements are made to investigate the effects of one or another drug on the pressures within the heart and lungs. Knowing these measurements is often of great benefit to me in planning treatment for the patient, and in fact a patient's participation in such a trial usually helps to determine whether a drug is potentially useful for treating his or her heart failure.

I think the key point here is that while clinical trials, investigational agents, and experimental drugs all sound very science-fiction-like, they are actually an everyday part of medical care in this country. By and large, they represent an opportunity for your doctor to give you a new treatment for your heart failure that may not be available to the general public for many years to come. With the safety and monitoring requirements of federal and local agencies these trials are conducted in a very safe and efficient way.

While I mentioned earlier that patients are frequently reluctant to enter clinical trials, I think the more common situation is the reverse. Some patients are so eager to get into clinical trials because there may be something new, something bigger and better, available for them that they are ready to rush into the trials without understanding all the potential risks and benefits. Here is an example: Recently, there was quite a bit of publicity surrounding the early release of a drug that was still undergoing some clinical trials. The sponsoring company had issued press releases, and information was appearing in the newspapers and on radio and TV about a new drug for heart failure. The information about this drug was so positive that one of my patients rushed into my office with a newspaper in his hand and insisted, "Doc, you've got to get this drug for me." He was so caught up in pursuing something newer and bigger and better that he failed to realize that he was already in one of the clinical trials on the drug and had been taking it for the past 2 years!

But enthusiasm can overtake caution in investigators and administrators as well. One of the new drugs being investigated for the treatment of heart failure was recently shown to be so good in improving patients' exercise tolerance and symptoms that the pharmaceutical company was able to convince the Food and Drug Administration to approve the drug before completion of a study showing whether or not the drug had an effect on overall mortality in heart failure patients. The drug was released and touted in the media as a major advance in the treatment of heart failure, only to be followed within a month or so by reports from clinical trials revealing an increased mortality among patients taking the drug. Probably the only thing worse than building up the hopes of a heart failure patient on the basis of premature claims is to suddenly remove hopes.

Current Investigational Drug Therapies for Heart Failure

I really cannot give a complete list of investigational treatments for heart failure. First of all, any list would be practically obsolete by the time this book is published, or certainly within a short time thereafter. Furthermore, there are so many areas of development that no list could ever be complete. However, there are several broad areas that have been concentrated on in the recent past. Since we know that the failing heart lacks the power to contract or squeeze, many of the companies developing drugs for heart failure have focused on those that increase the heart's capacity to perform this action. By and large, most of these drugs have produced ill effects. However, there are several new ones being developed that stimulate the heart's squeezing action in a safe and seemingly effective manner. Longer-term studies are under way now to determine how long these drugs continue to enhance the contractility of the heart and to make sure they are safe over a long period of time.

As we discussed earlier, many drug treatments for heart failure work by opening up the arteries and veins, and researchers are continuously searching for drugs that do so safely, efficiently and, ideally, by means of a once-a-day dosing regimen. Also, researchers are conducting clinical trials to investigate the effects of various combinations of drugs.

Alternative Drugs for Heart Failure

A recent *New England Journal of Medicine* article estimated that as many as one-third of Americans used some form of alternative health care within the past year. It would not be surprising to find that many patients with heart failure are also looking for alternative measures. Part of the question, of course, is how you define alternative medicine: for many years the approach taken by Dr. Dean Ornish—for example, using low-fat diets, exercise, and meditation to help reverse blockages in the coronary arteries—was viewed as an alternative approach. At any rate, alternative approaches are becoming more acceptable as mainstream medicine, in fact, insurance companies are beginning to pay for these kinds of treatments. Most alternative approaches to the treatment of heart failure deal with vitamins or minerals or substances that are purported to have a beneficial effect on the heart—usually with the support of good hard data to prove the point. Again, I am reluctant to give a catalog of current alternative approaches to treating heart failure because I am sure there are many I would miss.

One drug, called coenzyme Q10, or CoQ_{10}, has been around for many years and has been touted as improving the energetics of the failing heart. More than any other drug considered an alternative therapy for heart failure, CoQ_{10} has in fact undergone several clinical trials both in the United States and in Europe—with both positive and negative results. One of the problems I see is that most of the clinical trials with CoQ_{10} have not had the firm end points that other trials have, and I think this is certainly something that needs to be addressed. The other major problem is one I learned about from patients of mine who have wanted to try this therapy, namely, that this vitamin, which can be bought in health food stores, is quite expensive and, in fact, can cost as much or more than some of the conventional medications.

I am truly hopeful that promising alternative approaches can be investigated in good clinical trials so that their proponents can have the opportunity to establish a sound scientific basis for their claims and to answer the question of whether or not they are useful approaches for treating patients with heart failure. Hopefully, as the efficacy of alternative treatments is established, they will also become safer and more affordable for patients who need them.

Experimental Nonpharmacologic Approaches to Treating Heart Failure

As you have no doubt noticed, most of the attention on treating heart failure, aside from dietary restriction, has been on using drugs that have one effect or another on the heart. I would like to mention here two nonpharmaco- logic, or nondrug, approaches to treating heart failure that are gaining interest and that you may hear more about in the future.

For years patients who had heart failure were admon- ished to not exercise and in fact to restrict their lifestyles severely. While this may reduce the burden on the heart, it also produces a severe deconditioning of the heart, along with the remainder of the muscles in a patient's body. Surprisingly, studies showing the beneficial effects of exer- cise on patients with heart failure have been conducted only recently. Many heart failure experts now commonly encourage all our patients to stay as active as possible and in fact suggest an aggressive cardiac rehabilitation training program for many. Since many patients with heart failure are elderly and have been severely limited in their exercise abilities for a long time, the period of training or condi- tioning often takes much longer than would be expected for a sedentary but younger patient. Nevertheless, im- provements resulting from exercise training can be seen within a short period of time, and patients may continue to show signs of improvement even after 6 months or a year. So far, there is no ideal form of exercise, and, sur- prisingly, even very minimal activity has a significant ef- fect on improving a patient's symptoms and ability to exer- cise.

Since exercise training appears to be quite safe in pa- tients with heart failure and can usually be done without an expensive training program, I think it is one of the modalities we will hear more about and will apply more regularly to patients with advanced heart failure.

Another interesting nondrug way of treating heart failure is through the use of specialized pacemakers. On the basis of studies first done in Europe, it has been noted that the benefits of pacing the heart muscle to help synchronize contractions of the upper and lower chambers include improving the symptoms of heart failure, exercise tolerance, and perhaps even longer survival time. While this is still a highly experimental approach to treating patients with heart failure, I think it is fascinating since pacemakers today can be put in quite simply and often do not even require an overnight hospital stay. If there is any evidence that pacemaker therapy works for a significant number of patients with heart failure, I think we will see this becoming a more standard treatment approach, though probably used in conjunction with medication treatments.

As you can see, there are multiple opportunities and options within the experimental approaches for treating heart failure. As each day goes by, better and newer ideas are being developed to help attack the serious problem of heart failure. I think that because of the way our research systems operate in the United States, most patients who enter clinical trials are, by and large, allowing themselves the opportunity to try new and potentially ground-breaking treatments while exposing themselves to minimal risk. I think that patients, with the advice and counsel of their physicians, can find the proper match for themselves with an investigational drug or device and thus open up their options for treatment even more.

The following is a sample of a typical consent form provided to my patients for an investigational study. The form, however, does not replace a serious discussion with a doctor or nurse involved in the study, a discussion that should address all the issues surrounding the treatment being studied.

CONSENT TO PARTICIPATE IN A RESEARCH STUDY

Metoprolol in Dilated Cardiomyopathy (MDC): A Randomized Controlled Multicenter Trial

Investigator: Marc A. Silver, M.D.

Statement of Consent and Purpose of Study. You have a disease of the heart muscle that is called cardiomyopathy. This disease is responsible for symptoms of heart failure, which may include shortness of breath. Cardiomyopathy is a serious disorder that may severely limit a person's endurance or may result in premature death. Currently, there is no medical or surgical cure for this condition. Although conventional treatment is helpful in relieving some of the symptoms, there are certain patients who do not return to a normal or near-normal lifestyle. Some of these patients may benefit from newer forms of treatment. One of these agents, metoprolol, is in the class of drugs called beta blockers, which have been used to treat other forms of heart disease. Some patients with cardiomyopathy treated with this drug have had improved exercise tolerance in our experience. Other investigators have confirmed this observation as well as demonstrated improved survival. Our objectives are to determine how and why patients are improved with metoprolol therapy.

I, _____, voluntarily agree to continue my participation in a research study involving a currently available medication named metoprolol, which is a beta blocker used to treat high blood pressure, chest pains, and migraine headaches. Its use, however, is experimental in the treatment of cardiomyopathy and heart failure.

Procedures: I agree to take part in a research study that evaluates the action of a drug on my heart. Either metoprolol or placebo (sugar pill) will be selected by lottery for my treatment. The randomization process will be performed by computer from a central location in Sweden. The medication will be started at a very low dose. The dose will be increased eight to ten times over

6 to 8 weeks. After each increase in dose, Dr. Silver or his associates will examine me weekly for the initial 6 weeks and then at least monthly for 12 months.

Before I am accepted into this study, I will undergo a series of tests to evaluate my heart function to determine if I am eligible to participate in this study. These tests include electrocardiogram, chest X-ray, 24-hour Holter (heartbeat recording), echocardiogram (sound wave recording of heart), a MUGA scan, and blood tests (approximately $1/2$ tablespoon of blood). Some participants, in order to make sure they have cardiomyopathy, may have already had a cardiac catheterization and/or a heart biopsy. I understand that I may be asked to perform a treadmill test prior to the study and again at 6 and 12 months.

Risks and Discomforts: There are some risks involved in participating in this study. These include adverse effects of metoprolol, all of which are not yet known. The known side effects include, in some patients, a worsening of their shortness of breath or an accumulation of fluid. This usually responds to decreasing the dose of metoprolol or increasing the dose of water pills. More often, some patients may feel tired or listless and may experience mild gastrointestinal problems, slowing of the heart rate, lowered blood pressure, or wheezing. I realize that metoprolol is still an investigational drug for my condition and that unexpected side effects could occur.

Benefits: It is possible that my continuing participation in this investigation may be beneficial and that if I continue to take metoprolol, my symptoms of heart failure may improve, as has been seen with other patients.

Alternative Procedures: Alternative medical therapy approved for the treatment of my heart failure, and which may be chosen if I decide not to participate in this study, consists of noninvestigational drugs, such as captopril.

Confidentiality of Data: I hereby agree to allow my name and medical records to be made available to Dr. Silver and to the Food and Drug Administration for the purpose of evaluating the results of this study. I consent to the publication of any data that may result from this study provided my name and any identifying information is not included in such publication. Therefore, information that may be identified with me will be released only with my written permission or as required by law.

Compensation for Injury: I understand that in the event of physical injury resulting from the research procedures the Hospital will provide me with free emergency care, if such care is necessary. I also understand that if I wish, the Hospital will provide nonemergency medical care but that neither Dr. Silver nor the Hospital assumes any responsibility to pay for such care or to provide me with financial compensation.

Costs: I understand that my participation in this research is not expected to result in any additional costs to me beyond what would be normally expected for treatment of my condition.

Absence of Guarantee: Dr. Silver has not made or represented any guarantee to me as to the results that I may expect from participation in this study.

Right to Withdraw: I have been advised that Dr. Marc A. Silver will answer any questions I may have regarding this research study, research-related injury, and research subject rights; that I am free to withdraw my consent and discontinue participation at any time without penalty; and that standard medical treatment for my condition will remain available to me. I have also been advised that Dr. Silver may terminate my participation in the study if in his judgment this action would be in my best interest.

If I choose to withdraw from this study, I agree to consult with Dr. Silver regarding the consequences of my decision and to let him conduct an orderly termination procedure for ending my participation in this study.

Dr. Silver can be reached by telephone at the following numbers:

_____

_____

Any significant new findings that develop during the course of this research that may be related to me will be provided to me.

I have been given a copy of this consent form, I have read and understood it, and I have had my questions answered.

_____   _____

Patient's signature   Date

_____

Witness Name

_____

Witness Signature

Chapter 11

Food and Heart Failure

When I decided to write this book for patients, I swore that I would not have a chapter with menus and foods that heart failure patients can and cannot eat, because that is what so many "heart books" contain. Nor did I want to include one of those commonly available tables that list the sodium content of a variety of foods. However, on the basis of my patients' questions and daily concerns, I've decided to include some of this information (in addition to what's contained in Chapter 7).

It is really from the knowledge of the many concerned dietitians whom I have worked with over the years and of my superb nursing clinicians—all of whom seem to spend half their waking hours checking out the food labels in grocery stores and the menus of restaurants—that I have compiled most of this information. Since one of my primary goals is to get heart failure patients back to a more active, productive, and normal lifestyle and since that lifestyle includes dining out for many people, I am including in this chapter information on eating in restaurants, eating working lunches, and sharing meals with family and friends that will not cause regrets later. This information is certainly not meant to be totally inclusive, but it includes some of the common tips we pass on to our patients, advice I think all Americans would do well to heed. (There are excellent resources that address the issue of food and the heart, and many are mentioned in Appendix II.)

Where's the Salt?

There is a lot of confusion as to what exactly sodium or salt is. Sodium is a naturally occurring mineral and, as such, is found in a variety of the foods we eat as well as in many other sources, including medications, drinks, and even softened water. Salt is sodium combined with chloride, another mineral. By and large, the table salt we eat is about 40% sodium and 60% chloride. Most people get most of their sodium from salt. Sodium is absolutely essential for regulating many of the activities of the body and for keeping the fluid balance normal. We all need a certain amount of salt in our diet each day. It is estimated that the average person needs less than 500 milligrams of sodium per day, or approximately one-quarter of a teaspoon of salt. Unfortunately, most Americans end up consuming as much as 5,000 or 6,000 milligrams on a daily basis. Some experts recommend that the average American ingest no more than 3,000 milligrams of sodium a day, and in fact I tell most of my patients with heart failure that they should have no more than 2,000 milligrams a day (or even less for certain people).

In a moment we will talk about some of the foods that contain salt or sodium and some of the hidden sources of sodium, but for many people there really is no mystery as to why they consume 3,000 to 5,000 milligrams of sodium on a daily basis. In fact, the answer is in their hands.

These people are the heavy salt users, and we've all seen them; they are the ones who salt their food even before they taste it. This is a very bad habit, one that is commonly learned growing up, and it can cause all kinds of medical problems, including high blood pressure. One way people who have heart failure and who need to restrict their salt or sodium intake each day can make a major impact on their health is simply to limit use of the salt shaker. By adding no salt with a salt shaker people can usually reduce their sodium content by as much as a third or more of their daily intake. People frequently ask me if they can use a salt substitute instead of the salt shaker. If you read the labels of most salt substitutes, you will find that they are other chlorides, such as potassium chloride, which are also salts. A high intake of potassium can send the body's potassium balance out of whack, particularly if a person is taking drugs, such as any one of the angiotensin-converting enzyme inhibitors, that have a tendency to make the body retain potassium. For those who are taking diuretics that tend to make the body hold on to potassium, the use of such a salt substitute can really cause a serious, even life-threatening, problem. I therefore tell most of my patients to get in the habit of living without a salt shaker; usually, over a period of 1 or 2 months they are able to adjust to a diet that has a lower sodium content.

Salt by Any Other Name . . .

One of the things people with heart failure have to learn to do is to look at the label of all the food they eat or buy in the store to better determine what the sodium content is. Today, foods are increasingly labeled with nutritional information, including the exact milligram content of sodium in the food either per container or per serving, but this does not apply to every food. Clearly, when the label says salt, most people are aware that this means this food that has a certain amount of sodium in it. But what if the label says sodium alginate or sodium sulfite or sodium caseinate or disodium phosphate or sodium benzoate or sodium hydroxide? Those are all forms of sodium! Many of them are preservatives that are used in the foods, but they still count toward your daily sodium intake. Everyone is aware of monosodium glutamate, or MSG, which is commonly used as a seasoning in Chinese foods, but many people are not aware that other forms of sodium, such as sodium citrate (which is used as an antioxidant in baking), can cause similar problems. Careful attention to food labels, as well as more pressure from Americans to have foods labeled more completely and properly, will make the whole process of monitoring sodium intake simpler in the future.

It's a Jungle Out There

Manufacturers of processed foods have been quick to pick up on this interest of the American public in restricting sodium or salt in their diet. But it seems that rather than make an earnest effort to help Americans restrict the salt in their diet, manufacturers have come up with various terms that seem to confuse people more than anything else. The word *light* or *lite* is being used almost everywhere, and poor unsuspecting Americans are gobbling up these foods and imagining that they are getting lighter in weight and healthier with every bite. By and large, these "light" foods contain a smaller percentage of calories than an equivalent portion of a comparable product, but they make no other specific claims, particularly with regard to sodium content. In fact, some of the "light" products contain the highest sodium content I've seen around!

Another term that is being used is *low sodium,* and this generally refers to products that contain less than 140 milligrams of sodium per serving or per 100 grams of food. While these are generally better than equivalent products that are not low in sodium, consumers must recognize that they can still get into a lot of trouble eating just a few servings of these low-sodium foods. The designation *salt free* means that the food product contains less than 5 milligrams of sodium per serving. This truly is a restricted sodium food and probably is better than either the low-sodium or full-sodium products.

Since Americans get over 80% of the sodium they ingest each day from processed foods, it is almost better to stay away from processed foods altogether. For example, a lot of my patients make their own soups at home with no added salt, using only vegetables and chicken or meat. An 8-ounce bowl of homemade soup with no salt added either in the cooking process or at the table has no more than about 25 or 30 milligrams of sodium. But just half a can of a certain brand of processed chicken noodle soup has well over 1,000 milligrams of sodium. As a general rule, fresh fruits and vegetables and foods that are prepared in the home are far better for you than most processed foods or most restaurant foods.

Among common foods that many Americans seem to have trouble with are bread products. I learned a very important lesson 2 years ago when my wife and I bought a home bread machine for a Christmas present. We went to the book store and bought a wonderful book of recipes on making breads in our new machine. We were shocked, however, when we saw how much salt was added to most regular bread recipes. We gradually cut back further and further until we added no salt at all to the recipes, and—lo and behold—they tasted just as good and came out just as well. I think learning to live without salt in the diet is like most other conditions in life: one can grow accustomed to it in a relatively short period of time. In our home we do not have a salt shaker on the table—in fact, I haven't even seen it in well over 2 years! Our children do not use salt, and while they do like some salty snacks, they limit their consumption of them to rare occasions.

Another step to take is to learn which foods are high in sodium and which ones are low. For example, foods that are generally high in sodium—and by that I mean containing over 150 milligrams per serving—are, almost without exception, lunch meats (such as bologna or salami), hot dogs, bacon, cheese, canned soups, crackers, and pretzels. A good rule of thumb is to buy frozen instead of canned vegetables because salt is usually used as a preservative in the canning process. On the other hand, foods that have a lower sodium content, usually no more than 50 milligrams per serving, are fresh vegetables, fresh fruit, and pasta that has been cooked with little or no sodium in the water. And, yes, you can even eat popcorn that has not been salted.

Better Salt Substitutes

Whether it is truly a matter of taste or psychological, getting rid of all the salty flavor is too much for some people to bear. Fortunately, there are some excellent herbs and spices that are good alternatives for flavoring food, including some commercially prepared brands, such as Mrs. Dash and Papa Dash. However, I commonly tell people to use generous amounts of lemon juice or vinegar, particularly on top of vegetables and salads. Meats and vegetables can be cooked with mushrooms, mint leaves, green peppers, or even generous amounts of onions and garlic. Even cooking with fruit, for example, apricots and peaches, is an option. One of my patients became almost addicted to fresh horseradish when he found that that was the only thing that would allow him to beat the salt habit.

Go to your spice shelf and look at all those little bottles of spices you may have bought years ago and have never known what to do with. These spices can now become good substitutes for salt. Many of them—such as allspice, bay leaves, caraway seeds, garlic powder, marjoram, dry mustard, thyme, ginger, paprika, rosemary, sage, tarragon, basil, dill, and poppy seeds—can be used either at the table or during cooking to enhance the flavor of your food and get you out of the salt habit. Talk to your local nutritionist or your hospital dietitian for other suggestions on what to substitute for the high salt-containing foods in your diet.

The Big Hitters

Not too long ago a patient with whom my staff and I had spent a fair amount of time in the office going over salt and fluid restriction, as we normally do, decided that he wanted to tell me exactly what he had eaten one day of the previous weekend. Actually, I think he just wanted to see how much I could cringe. For lunch he went to a fast-food restaurant and ate a quarter-pound hamburger with cheese plus half a dozen dill pickles (the friends he ate with disliked the dill pickles that came on their sandwiches and gave them to my patient). He assured me that the pickles couldn't have been a problem because the fast food chain was getting so cheap that they were slicing the pickles very thin. Unfortunately, the burger with cheese was well over 1,100 milligrams of sodium, and when I told my patient that the dill pickles probably had the same amount of sodium as the entire hamburger, he thought I was simply picking on him. He thought I would be pleased to hear that for dinner he had chicken. Unfortunately, this was not a grilled or broiled breast of chicken but the Colonel's original-recipe fried chicken. I estimated that his serving probably added another 2,000 milligrams of sodium to his total for the day.

There are other foods that are also "big hitters" in the sodium league that you might not be aware of. One cup of potato salad can have as much as 1,300 milligrams of sodium, a chef's salad with ham and cheese on top can have 1,100 or 1,200, and spaghetti with meat sauce can have 1,000. Just to give you an idea of the range in the sodium content of foods, here are two tables, one (Table 11.1) listing some foods that have either a low or medium sodium content and the other (Table 11.2) listing those with high sodium content.

Table 11.3 lists a number of obvious and perhaps not so obvious foods of high sodium content. It would be wise to try to avoid these "big hitters."

TABLE 11.1. Foods with a Low to Medium Sodium Content

Food	Milligrams of sodium
Apple	2
Applesauce (1 cup)	6
Bread (one slice/white)	114
Butter (1 tbsp, salted)	116
Club soda (8 oz)	39
Fresh tuna (3 oz)	50
Margarine (1 tbsp)	140
Tomato	14
Water (8 oz tap)	12
White wine (4 oz)	19

Source: U.S. Department of Agriculture.

TABLE 11.2. Foods with High Sodium Content

Food	Milligrams of sodium
Antacid in water	564
Apple pie (1/8)	108
Canned tuna (3 oz)	384
Corn flakes (1 cup)	256
Cottage cheese (4 oz)	457
Dill pickle	928
English muffin	293
Salt (1 tsp)	1,938
Soy sauce (1 tbsp)	1,029
Tomato soup (1 cup)	932

Source: U.S. Department of Agriculture.

Dining Out

Without a doubt, my patients who eat more than one or two meals in a restaurant each week have the most difficult time controlling their consumption of sodium. People eat meals out nowadays for a variety of reasons. Some are busy and don't have time to prepare foods in their homes. I've been told that up to 60% of Americans eat lunch in a fast food restaurant, a dramatic shift even in the past decade. One of my patients is quite poor and lives in a YMCA hotel; he has no cooking facilities there and must eat all of his meals out, which means that it has been extremely hard for him to control the salt in his diet. Because of either their inability or an unwillingness to cook, the elderly tend to eat a lot of meals in restaurants (and very commonly in fast food restaurants because of the cost).

Whatever their reasons for frequent dining out, all patients with heart failure have to be aware that restaurants, particularly fast food restaurants, are danger signs along the road to feeling better. The following are some

TABLE **11.3.** Where the Sodium Is: The Big Hitters

Food	Milligrams of sodium
10¾ oz serving Campbell's Chunky Chicken Noodle Soup	1,140
1 McDonald's quarter pounder with cheese	1,110
4 oz Kellogg's All-Bran, dry	1,040
1 cup Jell-O Instant Chocolate Pudding	1,030
1 (6½ oz) can Chicken of the Sea Chunk Light Tuna in Spring Water, drained	994
1 Stouffer's French Bread Deluxe Pizza	950
1 tbsp Kikkoman Soy Sauce	938
1 medium dill pickle	928
1 Hardee's chef's salad, without dressing	910
2 oz Kraft Velveeta	860
1 cube Wyler Chicken Flavor Bouillon	850
½ cup Chef Boyardee Spaghetti Sauce with Mushrooms	845
3 Bisquick Original Mix pancakes	700
½ cup cooked Uncled Ben's Brown or Wild Rice	500
4 oz Light n' Lively Free Cottage Cheese	390
1 (4.3 oz) Hostess Apple Pie	370
1 tbsp Dijon mustard	360
3 cups Orville Redenbacher Natural Flavor Popcorn (for microwave)	330

tips you would be wise to follow when you eat out at a restaurant:

1. Before you go to the restaurant, try to find out if they serve a wide variety of foods rather than a specific form of food. For example, going to a restaurant that serves only deep-fried items is going to be a disaster. You might want to call ahead and see if they have the American Heart Association's Heart Healthy Diets on their menu. A quick call to

the restaurant, even anonymously, can save you embarrassment once you're there and discomfort after you've eaten your meal there.

2. Once you get to the restaurant, take your time and look carefully at the menu. Be sure to ask the waiter or waitress how the food is prepared if you are in doubt. See if foods can be prepared without salt, and choose foods that have the lowest sodium content.

3. As an appetizer get either a fruit-containing item, fruit juice, or a vegetable, rather than a pasta or baked item.

4. For your entree order something that can be roasted, broiled, or grilled without adding any extra salt. Fish or fresh meats are good choices. Pasta—if you can get it without the sauce, say, with a little garlic and oil—is probably better for you than something like a breaded veal cutlet.

5. Avoid sauces and gravies at all costs. These are usually high in sodium and will only get you into trouble. Also avoid breaded items, which are also high in salt or sodium content. When you order a salad, try to use a low-sodium salad dressing, if one is available, or—better yet—use vinegar and oil on your salad. And try to use the separate vinegar and oil containers rather than the combinations, which may be commercially prepared and may have a high sodium content.

What should you do if all else fails and you're in a situation where there's virtually nothing on the menu that you can eat that does not have some sodium in it? I recommend that you simply cut down on your portion size and realize that for the next day or so your sodium restriction is going to have to be even more strict. Despite all that, I must say that eating out today is easier for the heart failure patient than it was before because of the acceptance of patrons' dietary restrictions and flexibility of most restaurants. I think it helps most, however, to be thoroughly familiar with foods that are high in sodium so that you can avoid them and make more intelligent selections from a menu. Presented in Table 11.4 are some of the foods typically eaten for breakfast, lunch, and dinner in restaurants (or, for that matter, at home), along with their sodium content. Table 11.5 lists selections from the major sections of a restaurant menu that are recommended and those you are advised to avoid.

Since many of our patients do eat in fast-food restaurants, in Table 11.6 I "name names" and show you exactly what the sodium content is for most of these foods. As you can see, there are very few low-sodium foods you can get in a fast-food restaurant.

Food plays an important role in our lives; we eat not only for sustenance but also to fulfill social and business rites. Many patients develop heart disease due, in part, to their dietary habits. In general, something that is restricted takes on more attention and importance, but I believe that most patients can and do readily adapt to a low sodium diet. For some patients, following charts and recipes is the only way to maintain the diet; others grasp the general notion and can stay well within their limits on a daily basis. It is critical however, for patients and families to accept the necessity of dietary restrictions based on an understanding of the disease. Finally, patients and their families must make sure that the diet does not control them or adversely affect their lives and, instead, should take the perspective that diet is yet another aspect of life that they can control, enjoy, and from which they can benefit.

TABLE 11.4. Sodium Content of Common Foods

Food item	Milligrams of sodium
Breakfast	
Bacon, pork (2 strips)	202
Bagel with 1 oz cream cheese	283
Bran muffin	168
Coffee, brewed (1 cup)	8
Coffee cake (1 piece)	310
Cornflakes (1 cup) with low-fat milk	361
Corn muffin	192
Danish pastry, plain	249
Doughnut, plain	139
English muffin	358
French toast (2 slices)	514
Fried egg, large (1)	162
Fruit yogurt, low-fat (1 cup)	133
Grapefruit, half	0
Hash browns (1 cup)	54
Link sausages, pork (2)	336
Oatmeal, cooked (1 cup)	1
Orange juice, frozen (1 cup)	2
Pancakes (2)	320
Tea, brewed (1 cup)	8
Toast, wheat (1 slice)	153
Tomato juice, canned (1 cup)	882
Two-egg omelet, ham and cheese	598
Lunch	
Cheeseburger, fast food	750
Cheese pizza (1 slice)	261
Chef's salad, ham and cheese (1 cup)	1,134
Chicken noodle soup (1 cup)	1,107
Chicken noodle soup, low-sodium (1 cup)	36
Cola (12 oz)	12
Coleslaw ($\frac{1}{2}$ cup)	16
Corn chips (1 oz)	164
Cottage cheese, low-fat (1 cup)	918

(*continued*)

TABLE 11.4. (*Continued*)

Food item	Milligrams of sodium
Diet cola (12 oz)	24
Dill pickle (1 medium)	928
French fries (20), unsalted	30
Fruit salad (1 cup)	9
Green salad, tossed (1 cup)	53
Ham and cheese sandwich	792
Hamburger, fast food	500
Hot dog on bun	671
Potato chips (14 chips)	164
Potato salad (1 cup)	1,323
Roast beef sandwich	792
Tomato, whole (1)	10
Tuna salad (1 cup)	434
Vegetable beef soup (1 cup)	957
Vegetable soup, low-sodium (1 cup)	38
Dinner	
Beef burrito, fast food	746
Beef or pork chop suey, homemade (1 cup)	1,052
Beer (12 oz)	24
Broccoli, raw/boiled (1 cup)	16
Broiled codfish (1 fillet)	141
Broiled pork chop	49
Broiled sirloin steak (4 oz)	74
Chicken chow mein, homemade (1 cup)	717
Chili con carne (1 cup)	135
Dinner roll	144
Fettuccine Alfredo, frozen (1 portion)	1,195
Fish sticks (4 oz)	651
Fried chicken breast	385
Green beans, french, frozen (1 cup)	17
Light beer (12 oz)	12
Macaroni and cheese, homemade (1 cup)	1,086
Peas and carrots, frozen/boiled (1 cup)	110
Potato, peeled and boiled	7

(*continued*)

TABLE 11.4. (*Continued*)

Food item	Milligrams of sodium
Red wine (4 oz)	76
Rice, cooked (1 cup)	4
Roast chicken breast	138
Roast turkey breast, without skin (1 cup)	89
Spaghetti with tomato–meat sauce (1 cup)	1,009
White wine (4 oz)	72
Desserts	
Angel food cake (1 slice)	142
Apple pie (1 slice)	207
Banana	1
Brownie with nuts (1)	50
Cheesecake (1 slice)	189
Chocolate chip cookies (2)	76
Chocolate pudding (1 cup)	335
Devil's food cake with chocolate icing (1 slice)	180
Fresh pineapple (1 cup)	1
Fresh strawberries (1 cup)	2
Hot fudge sundae (2 scoops)	190
Lemon meringue pie (1 slice)	223
Oatmeal-raisin cookies (2)	74
Orange sherbet ($\frac{1}{2}$ cup)	44
Pound cake (1 slice)	58
Rice pudding with raisins (1 cup)	188
Vanilla ice cream ($\frac{1}{2}$ cup)	58
Yellow cake with white icing (1 slice)	191
Condiments	
Barbecue sauce ($\frac{1}{4}$ cup)	508
Brown gravy ($\frac{1}{4}$ cup)	31
Butter, regular (1 pat)	41
Butter, unsalted (1 pat)	< 1
Catsup (1 tbsp)	156
Cream cheese (1 tbsp)	85
Hollandaise sauce ($\frac{1}{4}$ cup)	284

(*continued*)

TABLE 11.4. (*Continued*)

Food item	Milligrams of sodium
Italian dressing (1 tbsp)	116
Italian dressing, low-calorie (1 tbsp)	118
Margarine (1 pat)	47
Mayonnaise (1 tbsp)	104
Mushroom gravy ($\frac{1}{4}$ cup)	340
Mustard, prepared (1 tbsp)	195
Pancake syrup (2 tbsp)	70
Parmesan cheese (1 tbsp)	116
Soy sauce (1 tbsp)	1,029
Thousand Island dressing (1 tbsp)	109
Thousand Island dressing, low-calorie (1 tbsp)	153
White sauce ($\frac{1}{4}$ cup)	199
Worcestershire sauce (1 tbsp)	147

TABLE 11.5. Dining Out: What to Order and What to Avoid

Menu section	Recommended	Not recommended (too high in fat and/or sodium)
Appetizers	Fruit juice	Soups, especially cream style
	Fresh or canned fruit	Fried vegetables or potato skins
	Gelatin	Vegetable juices
	Relish plates (with raw vegetables)	Relish plates (with preserved or pickled items)
Salads	Fresh vegetable salad served with lemon, vinegar, or low-calorie dressing	Coleslaw

(*continued*)

TABLE 11.5. (*Continued*)

Menu section	Recommended	Not recommended (too high in fat and/or sodium)
	Sliced tomatoes	Macaroni or potato salad
	Fruit salad	Salad with excessive amounts of salad dressing
	Gelatin salad	Cottage cheese
Entrees	Any lean meat, fish, or poultry that has been roasted, baked, boiled, or poached	Stews and casserole-type dishes
		Fatty, fried, or breaded meats
		Eggs
Vegetables	Stewed, steamed, or boiled	Those in a sauce or au gratin
		Seasoned with butter or cooked in egg yolk batter
		Fried vegetables
Potatoes and substitutes	Mashed, baked, boiled, or steamed potatoes	Fried potatoes
	Boiled or steamed rice	Creamed or au gratin potatoes
	Boiled noodles	Fried rice
		Noodles in a cream sauce
Breads	Hard or soft rolls	Crescents, butter rolls, popovers, and croissants
	Plain bread or toast	Sweet rolls, cakes, or coffee cake

(*continued*)

TABLE 11.5. (*Continued*)

Menu section	Recommended	Not recommended (too high in fat and/or sodium)
	Unsalted crackers Breadsticks or melba toast Matzos and plain toast	Salted crackers or breads
Condiments	Low-calorie salad dressing Oil and vinegar (use oil sparingly)	Excess gravy Fried or creamed items Butter or cream Sour cream Cream cheese Bacon Mayonnaise-type salad dressing Cheese sauces
Desserts	Fresh fruit Angel food cake Sherbet or Italian ice Fruit sorbet or frozen nonfat or lowfat yogurt Ice milk Gelatin	Pastries, cakes, and cream pies Chocolate Ice cream
Beverages	Fruit juice Skim milk Soft drinks Tea or coffee, preferably decaffeinated	Milk shakes Chocolate milk Whole milk Cocoa Alcohol (unless allowed by physician)

TABLE 11.6. Sodium Content of Fast Food

Menu item	Portion	Milligrams of sodium
Kentucky Fried Chicken		
Original Recipe		
Wing	1	387
Center breast	1	532
Drumstick	1	269
Thigh	1	517
Extra-Crispy Recipe		
Wing	1	437
Center breast	1	842
Drumstick	1	346
Thigh	1	766
Buttermilk biscuits	1	521
Mashed potatoes with gravy	1	297
Coleslaw	1	171
McDonald's		
Egg McMuffin	1	740
Hot cakes with butter and syrup	1	640
Scrambled eggs	1	290
Pork sausage	1	350
Hash brown potatoes	1	330
Biscuit with sausage and egg	1	1,250
Hamburger	1	500
Cheeseburger	1	750
Quarter Pounder	1	718
Big Mac	1	950
Filet-O-Fish	1	1,030
McDLT	1	990
Chicken McNuggets	6 pieces	520
Chef salad	1	490
Chunky chicken salad	1	230
French fries	1 small	110

(*continued*)

TABLE 11.6. (*Continued*)

Menu item	Portion	Milligrams of sodium
Apple pie	1	240
Vanilla shake	1	170
Chocolate shake	1	240
Strawberry shake	1	170
McDonaldland cookies	1	300
Chocolate chip cookies	1	280
Pizza Hut		
(All portions are based on two slices of medium pizza.)		
Pan Pizza		
Cheese		940
Pepperoni		1,127
Supreme		1,363
Super Supreme		1,447
Thin 'n Crispy Pizza		
Cheese		867
Pepperoni		867
Supreme		1,328
Super Supreme		1,336
Personal Pan Pizza		
Pepperoni	1 whole	1,335
Supreme	1 whole	1,313
Subway		
Subway Club	1	839
Turkey Sub	1	839
Tuna Sub	1	905
Steak Sub	1	883
Meatball Sub	1	876
Ham Sub	1	839
Roast Beef Sub	1	839
Seafood and Crab Sub	1	1,306
Subway chef salad without dressing	1	479

(*continued*)

TABLE 11.6. (*Continued*)

Menu item	Portion	Milligrams of sodium
Taco Bell		
Taco	1	276
Taco Light	1	594
Soft Taco	1	516
Soft Taco Supreme	1	516
Tostada	1	596
Taco salad with salsa	1	1,286
Taco salad without shell	1	1,056
Steak fajitas	1	485
Chicken fajitas	1	619
Wendy's		
Omelet #3: Ham, cheese, onion, green pepper	1	485
Omelet #4: Mushroom, onion, green pepper	1	200
Breakfast sandwich	1	770
French toast	2 slices	850
$\frac{1}{4}$ lb single hamburger on white bun	1	360
$\frac{1}{4}$ lb bacon cheeseburger on white bun	1	780
Frosty (medium)	12 oz	220
Plain baked potato	1	60
Baked potato with chili and cheese	1	610
White Castle		
Hamburger	1	266
Cheeseburger	1	361
Fish sandwich without tartar sauce	1	201
Chicken sandwich	1	497
Sausage and egg sandwich	1	698
Sausage sandwich	1	488
Arby's		
Roast beef	1	588
Beef and cheddar	1	955

(*continued*)

TABLE 11.6. (Continued)

Menu item	Portion	Milligrams of sodium
Ham and cheese	1	1,350
Chicken breast sandwich	1	1,082
Turkey deluxe	1	1,047
Potato cakes	1	397
Burger King		
Breakfast Croissan'wich Cheese	1	607
Breakfast Croissan'wich Bacon	1	719
Breakfast Croissan'wich Sausage	1	985
Breakfast Croissan'wich Ham	1	962
Scrambled egg platter		
Egg, croissant, hash browns	1	893
Egg, with sausage	1	1,271
Egg, with bacon	1	1,043
French toast sticks	1	537
Great Danish	1	288
Bagel sandwich		
Egg and cheese	1	759
Egg and bacon	1	872
Egg and sausage	1	1,137
Egg and ham	1	1,114
Milk, 2%	8 oz	122
Milk, whole	8 oz	119
Whopper	1	865
Whopper with Cheese	1	1,177
Bacon Double Cheeseburger	1	748
Mushroom Swiss Double Burger	1	795
Hamburger	1	505
Cheeseburger	1	661
Cheeseburger Deluxe	1	652
Hamburger Deluxe	1	496
Chicken Broiler Sandwich	1	746

(continued)

TABLE 11.6. (*Continued*)

Menu item	Portion	Milligrams of sodium
Chicken Tenders	1	54
Chef salad	1	568
Chicken Chunkey Salad	1	443
Thousand Island dressing	2 oz	403
French dressing	2 oz	400
Ranch dressing	2 oz	316
Olive oil and vinegar	2 oz	214
Reduced-calorie Italian dressing	2 oz	762

Chapter 12

Other Forms of Treatment for Heart Failure

In previous chapters I discussed conventional as well as experimental treatments for heart failure and addressed the topic of heart transplantation. These are the primary medical and surgical approaches to treating patients with heart failure. In this chapter I want to talk about an additional treatment: a drug treatment that is given in an intermittent form either in the patient's home or in an outpatient setting such as a heart failure center or hospital. Later in the chapter I discuss some important adjunctive treatments for heart failure: supplemental oxygen and elastic support stockings.

Intermittent Infusions

One of the treatments your doctor may use when your heart muscle gets particularly weak is intravenous administration of a drug to help the heart pump stronger. Several such drugs are on the market, including dobutamine, amrinone, and milrinone. One or more of these might well be the drug your doctor would turn to should you be admitted to the hospital in serious heart failure and retaining large amounts of fluid. Helping the heart to pump stronger, these drugs work with diuretics to help clear your body of the excess fluid you are retaining; they may well make you feel better rapidly, and they certainly help to compensate your heart failure. Although some patients need to get these drugs on a continuous basis in order to be able to go home from the hospital, it is more common today for doctors to use these drugs in an intermittent fashion for patients who are frequently admitted to the hospital to clear the fluid from their body. A doctor may decide to use intermittent infusion with a patient who is on a downward course, for example, one who has had one or two heart failure admissions over the past couple of years, who is now beginning to retain more fluid despite increasing doses of the diuretics, and who has had perhaps increasing hospital admissions within a period of months. One of the doctor's goals is certainly to improve how the patient feels, another is to limit the number of hospitalizations. Thus, the doctor may choose to give this patient intermittent infusions of drugs to help control the heart failure—in a sense, to prevent marked worsening of the heart failure—and to therefore prevent recurrent hospitalizations.

Let me say at the outset that despite increasingly widespread use of these intermittent infusions there has been no evidence that they prolong the life of patients who have very serious heart failure. A patient who is at the point of requiring frequent infusions has very advanced heart failure; obviously, the long-term prognosis may not be very good. On the other hand, I think doctors who have had broad experience using infusions feel that this procedure does certainly limit the number of recurrent hospitalizations and that it can support a patient during a difficult period (when there is more heart failure) and allow the physician to try other therapies afterward that may even allow the patient to come off the infusions completely.

There are many issues regarding the use and abuse of intravenous infusions of *inotropic* (that is, affecting muscle contractility) drugs, issues that are still being sorted out in the professional literature. However, I think that there are some common issues that patients should be aware of.

There are two common drug types that are used for these kinds of infusions. It will certainly be up to your doctor to decide which one is best for you, but I think one of the important aspects of these infusion treatments is that the choice of drug be made in a more or less scientific fashion. Under the best circumstances, the drug chosen will be one that has definitely been shown to improve a particular individual's heart function. There is a lot of variability in patients' responses to these drugs; that is, a drug may work perfectly well for one patient but not at all for another. Commonly, we test the drugs when a patient is hospitalized and has a Swan-Ganz catheter in place, which can tell us about how the heart and lung pressures respond to a dose of a drug. We also know, however, that a patient's acute response in the hospital may not predict his or her more chronic response after leaving the hospital. In fact, a patient who responds well to Drug X in the hospital may later cease responding to that drug. Nonetheless, testing the drug while the patient is hospitalized with a Swan-Ganz catheter in place is very useful in determining which drug he or she should get as an outpatient.

Another valid way to select the right drug to use is to observe what we call the "clinical response," that is, the patient's response to an intervention, which in this case is how well the patient does in getting rid of fluid while he or she is on the drug. However, when patients are hospitalized, they receive several therapies at one time, including diuretics, bed rest, and salt and fluid restriction, recommendations to which they may not have strictly adhered at home. These therapies may falsely lead the physician to believe that it is the particular intravenous drug that is working wonders for the patient when, in fact, the patient's improvement may be due to the enforced adherence to these basic components of conventional care. Nevertheless, most physicians can determine when a drug has accelerated or improved the patient's course and can use that clinical information to decide which drug the patient should receive for further infusions.

Unfortunately, not all physicians are familiar with how to administer and assess the effects of these kinds of drugs, and some end up using only what they are most familiar with or learned about during their training. I believe that that is unfair to the patient; as I said earlier, there should be some scientific basis for choosing a particular drug. You should also know that this is a rather controversial area and that there are some physicians who feel that there is no clear role for these intravenous drugs.

How Often to Get the Treatments and for How Long

Another rather unclear area regarding infusions is how long the outpatient intermittent infusions should be. Normally, when patients are in the hospital, they get these intravenous inotropic drugs continuously for one or more days, but at some point a decision has to be made about how often an individual should get them as an outpatient and with what frequency. Most patients end up getting the infusions once a week, or at most, two or three times a week. This is a somewhat arbitrary decision but one that should be based on the particular patient's ability to be weaned off the drug prior to discharge from the hospital, as well as on frequent clinical assessment by the physician. If a patient is able to come off a drug completely and leave the hospital but the physician is concerned that he or she may need the drug again to prevent a recurrence of the heart failure, then it will be necessary to check the patient quite closely even within a day or two after discharge from the hospital. If there are early signs of reaccumulation of fluid (weight gain or increased shortness of breath, for example), the patient may be a candidate for infusion at least once or twice during the subsequent week in order to prevent a rehospitalization. Some patients need infusions almost constantly, and in those situations everything should be done to try to improve the patient's overall status. Other patients end up getting infusions approximately once a week and then after a period of stability are weaned down to once every other week, with some patients even getting by with infusions once every 3 or 4 weeks. In my general experience, once patients can be weaned down to once every other week, they usually tell you that they don't feel much different after the infusions; at that point, the procedure can be discontinued, either on a permanent or a temporary basis.

Another decision to make involves the duration of an individual infusion procedure. I've seen infusions given for anywhere from 3 to about 72 hours, with some physicians in the latter case admitting their patients on a Friday afternoon and keeping them until late in the day on Sunday for what they call an "inotrope holiday." I think this extended infusion should be reserved for the most refractory of patients. It certainly sounds like anything but a holiday to me! I generally give my patients about 6 hours of treatment when they need it, since that tends to work out well from a scheduling perspective and also, I think, allows an ample infusion of the medication. Shorter periods do not give ample time for the drug to give its full benefit. However, I admit that decisions about infusions are purely judgment calls; there's very little technical information to say that one protocol or duration is better than another.

Where Infusions Are Given

As I mentioned earlier, infusions can be given with patients being either temporary inpatients in the hospital or outpatients either at home or in a variety of settings. Many hospitals have patients come in for a stay of 4, 6, or 8 hours in their emergency department or on one of the telemetry (monitoring) floors. I have those sorts of telemetry outpatient arrangements at a couple of hospitals, and they have worked reasonably well. I also have had a dedicated area within my office, which is a more ideal situation because the patient's progress can be directly monitored, the patients get intensive care and education directly from our nurses, and I get to examine patients and monitor their progress each time they come.

Probably one of the more common modes of delivering this therapy has been its administration in the home by one of the many home nursing agencies. In the interests of keeping patients out of the hospital, there has been a marked upsurge in the use of therapies utilizing home nursing services. I have found a wide range of variability both in the skills and the goals of these nursing services and have therefore found wide variability in the kind of care patients with heart failure get in their home. It makes little sense to me to take some of the sicker patients, who have very advanced heart failure and who need to be seen frequently with close monitoring, and place them in a home setting with perhaps the least amount of monitoring. I think many physicians choose this option for patients who have recurrent admissions because they think there is little hope or little else to do for those patients. With rare exception, I think that infusion at home is usually not the most ideal situation for the end-stage patient. This is very much a point of personal perspective. Many doctors do use these infusions as a sort of end-stage treatment for patients who have not responded to conventional treatments. I personally view them as a very temporary situation to help patients over a period of decompensation or to get them onto other, perhaps newer, conventional and/or investigational drugs. In fact, from the moment I start a patient on an intermittent course of infusions my goal is to find a way to eventually get him or her off. Frequently, when I go to an institution that has been doing infusions for a while I almost always find patients who have been getting this treatment weekly for as long as 2 years, or perhaps more. I generally find that at least half of these patients could easily come off the infusions with simply some adjustments in their medications, and sometimes even with little or no change whatsoever.

Since there has been such a proliferation of home care agencies, I would like to suggest a few criteria for selecting such an agency for a heart failure patient:

1. The agency should have expertise in treating heart disease *and* heart failure. Several agencies have chosen to concentrate their focus in these areas.
2. The agency should have a cadre of expertly trained nurses who are interested in heart failure. I rou-

tinely invite home care nurses to my office so that I can assess the level of knowledge and interest they have and teach them points I think are important.

3. The agency should have good communications with your doctor. The staff need to be able to transmit lab results, convey anything they notice in the home back to the doctor, and carry out instructions. They must serve as the doctor's eyes and ears.

4. The agency should have definite goals and targets in mind, as should the doctor, in order to help the patient become more self-reliant and return to a greater level of independence.

Potential Adverse Effects from Intermittent Infusions

As I mentioned earlier, there is no clearly proven benefit, in terms of increased survival, for patients who get infusions. While there has been some suggestion that the use of these drugs on a regular basis may actually shorten survival, there is no clear proof for that statement either.

In order to get these drugs intravenously on a regular basis, patients must either have an intravenous catheter placed each time the treatment is given or have a more permanent form of catheter introduced into the body. The latter is what we call a central line, or a catheter that is usually buried under the skin and that is inserted into a large vein in the body. There are several kinds of these central line catheters, including Hickman, Groshong, Port-A-Cath, triple lumen, and PICC catheters. All have their advantages and disadvantages, and most require surgical placement. A permanent catheter can be well maintained but increases the risk of infection, which can certainly be a very serious problem for the patient who already has heart failure.

There are also risks from the infusion procedure, including an increase in irregular heartbeats because of an increase in the irritability of the heart; large shifts in the electrolytes, that is, in the sodium or potassium in the patient's blood; episodes of low blood pressure; and occasional allergic reactions to the drugs themselves.

In summary, the intermittent infusion of inotropic drug—when selected judiciously and used in appropriate patients in the appropriate setting for an appropriate interval of time—is a common, useful technique for at least improving the quality of life for many patients with heart failure.

Supplemental Oxygen

One of the most frequent questions I get from patients and their families is whether or not the patient with heart failure should have an oxygen supply in the home. This usually involves a two-part answer. Since the weak heart and congested lungs frequently have a difficult time getting enough oxygen into the blood circulation or delivering enough oxygen to the rest of the body, it seems logical that supplementing the oxygen supply would make the patient feel better. In fact, this is true, and it's one of the first treatments we frequently give when we treat patients in the hospital. Moreover, oxygen can be considered a drug in that it has important effects on opening up the arteries and lowering the pressures within the lungs.

On the other hand, I have all too frequently seen patients with heart failure who are slowly getting worse over a period of days or weeks take to using their home oxygen on a regular basis only to appear in the emergency room with very severe heart failure. I think a false reliance on oxygen as a means of feeling better for the short term often backfires: it lets the patient get progressively sicker before calling the doctor and often results in a longer hospital stay. I have even seen patients rely on using their oxygen at home to such an extent that they limit their exercise because they are tethered to the oxygen cord.

Your doctor can do certain tests to help decide whether or not oxygen will be useful for you to use or have in your home. You should be aware that Medicare has very stringent criteria for those who qualify for home oxygen, and if you do not meet these qualifications, you may end up paying a hefty bill for oxygen use in your home.

Elastic Support Stockings

Many patients who have had bypass surgery are given a pair of white elastic stockings to wear after their surgery. These stockings provide continuous compression to the legs and act as a mechanical means of stimulating the blood return from the legs back to the heart. This same situation applies in patients with heart failure, and the elastic stockings can certainly provide a great deal of comfort and support for patients who have leg edema. These stockings should usually reach above the knee because the lower ones can constrict the return of fluid at the knee and may not eliminate the swelling of the legs. There are various kinds of elastic stockings available, but usually your hospital, pharmacy, or hospital supply company can recommend a good brand for you. Since leg swelling tends to diminish at night, when people are lying flat, it is generally best to put these stockings on the very first thing in the morning. If they are fitted properly, they should not be difficult to get on; however, the process may represent a good deal of effort for the patient with heart failure, and often the help of a spouse or other relative is needed. As the swelling in the legs subsides, the stockings may become loose, in which case patients may want to either go without them or get a better-fitting pair. And if more swelling develops in the legs, the stockings may become uncomfortable to wear and should then be avoided.

I have certainly found that support stockings are an important adjunct for many patients who continue to have lower leg swelling, and they are often a worthwhile investment for my patients.

Chapter 13

Quality of Life

On the occasion of his 90th birthday party, Senator Strom Thurmond of South Carolina had many people express wishes that they hoped to be able to attend his 100th birthday party. He said to them that if they ate the proper diet and exercised, they might be able to be there!

—National Public Radio

Two years ago I couldn't make a piece of toast; last Sunday I cooked dinner for sixteen.

—Patient A. P.

PATIENT R. P. (age 73): "Hey, Doc, I want to be able to go to my granddaughter's wedding."
DR. SILVER: "Oh, when is that?"
PATIENT R. P.: "Eighteen years from now."

The Golden Years? What's that? It seems someone forgot the G.

—A patient's spouse

In treating patients with heart failure there are obviously many goals, not just increased longevity. Since patients with heart failure are limited in their activity because of shortness of breath and fatigue, an additional goal would be to ameliorate these symptoms. Another goal is to improve the patient's quality of life. I must say that this is not a topic to which I pay mere lip service but, in fact, one of the primary goals I have in mind for each and every one of my patients. It is clear that the overall quality of life for those patients whose heart failure is so advanced and who have suffered for so long is not going to change significantly regardless of the treatment we could offer them. This is particularly true for the elderly patient with heart failure. Also, there are very limited treatments to make the very sickest patients feel completely well again, and therefore the focus really must be on quality of life.

One of the problems that arises when we address the subject of quality of life is, of course, how to define it and, even more difficult, how to measure it. In recent years there have been some major advances toward trying to quantify or measure the quality of life for patients with heart failure. This has been extremely important, for we can now, finally, evaluate how the various treatments we try for our patients with heart failure affect not only what we doctors call "end points," such as death or hospitalization, but also the quality of a patient's life. Thanks to people like Dr. Thomas Rector and Dr. Jay Cohn at the University of Minnesota, the Living With Heart Failure Questionnaire (page 191) has been developed and rigorously tested to show that it really is a valid instrument for measuring the quality of life in patients with heart failure. As you can see from the questions, this questionnaire touches on many of the common limitations patients with heart failure have and gives us good insight into both the physical and the emotional, or psychological, component of a patient's heart failure.

Living with Heart Failure Questionnaire

Did your heart failure prevent you from living as you wanted during the last month by:

1. causing swelling in your ankles?
2. making working around the house or yard difficult?
3. making relating to or doing things with your friends or family difficult?
4. making you sit or lie down to rest during the day?
5. making you tired, fatigued, or low on energy?
6. making working to earn a living difficult?
7. making walking about or climbing stairs difficult?
8. making you short of breath?
9. making sleeping well at night difficult?
10. making you eat less of the foods you like?
11. making going places away from home difficult?
12. making sexual activities difficult?
13. making recreational pastimes, sports, or hobbies difficult?
14. making it difficult for you to concentrate or remember things?
15. giving you side effects from medications?
16. making you worry?
17. making you feel depressed?
18. costing you money for medical care?
19. making you feel a loss of self-control?
20. making you stay in a hospital?
21. making you feel you are a burden to your family or friends

Many years ago, before such questionnaires were used for patients with heart failure, I asked a group of my patients who had all been in a drug trial and had received an experimental medication to fill out a form with some questions on it, namely, how they learned about their heart failure, which sources of information were helpful, and how they felt about being asked to join a drug study. I also surveyed them on their knowledge of the other treatments that were available. Many of the patients indicated that they now knew quite a bit about their heart failure; had learned primarily from talking with physicians, staff, and other patients; felt privileged to participate in a drug trial and felt they had received special care because of their participation; and so on. At the end of the questionnaire I left an open space, inviting patients to indicate anything else they thought I should know about them or about how their heart failure had affected their life. One man in his forties, who had heart failure for some time before he came to see me, wrote, "Not hardly anything except no work, no sex, no beer, and no money!" This would have amounted to a poor score on any quality-of-life questionnaire, and it certainly made an impression on me. I have never forgotten that if I haven't improved a person's quality of life, I haven't treated that person completely.

There are various other measurement tools available to assess a patient's quality of life, including the Heart Failure Functional Status Inventory, the Multiple Affect Adjective List, and the Psychosocial Adaptation to Illness Scale, to name a few. It is interesting to note that some of the objective measurements we make on a patient with heart failure, such as ejection fraction, very commonly bear little correlation to quality-of-life measurements. And probably an even more important observation is the conclusion from a recent study, namely, that the patient's baseline quality of life correlated significantly with overall longevity. Now you might say that this simply reflects the fact that the patients who felt better initially were the ones who lived longer, but I think this could also be interpreted to reflect the notion that patients with a better mental attitude and quality of life do better and survive longer despite an initial poor functional status. As Dr. Bernie Siegel says in *Love, Medicine, and Miracles*, "Exceptional patients have the ability to throw statistics aside—to say, 'I can be a survivor'—even when the doctor isn't wise enough to do so."

Look again at the third quotation at the beginning of this chapter. It was from a 73-year-old gentleman whom I was seeing for the first time. He was very sick with heart failure and, in fact, had quite limited physical capacity. He had just been discharged from a long hospitalization and was coming to my office to see if he could find a way to improve his heart failure and stay out of the hospital. It was at the end of my conversation with him that he made clear to me his goal of going to his granddaughter's wedding. I fell for his joke but I am happy to report that he is today doing well and that now his granddaughter's wedding is only 17 years away!

I mention this story because on the very same day I saw another gentleman with equally severe heart failure. This gentleman was coming to me from another cardiologist to see what we could offer him for his advanced heart failure. I in fact gave him almost the same options I gave the first patient, and he said he would consider them all and get back to me within the next couple of days. I was deeply disturbed late that evening to get a phone call from one of the emergency rooms reporting that this patient had been admitted with a self-inflicted gunshot wound. I found out later that this man had a rather long history of depression and that this was not his first suicide attempt. However, I think these two cases suggest that these two patients, despite equal severity of disease, felt quite differently about the quality of their life and viewed the same options differently—so differently that their view affected their approach to getting more help. And so even initial quality of life may influence how a patient accepts and responds to the idea of treatment for heart failure.

In fact, it is always one of my goals to try to assess the patient's quality of life right from the very outset and to try to make major changes in his or her quality of life even prior to attempting to make major improvements in his or her functional status. A recent study found that up to 43% of patients with advanced heart failure had feelings of depression, hostility, and anger because of their limited daily activity. We often find that very simple changes make big differences in the quality of life and help motivate people to stick with their treatments. An example of this is simply changing the second diuretic dose to about 4 in the afternoon rather than 9 or 10 at night, thus allowing people to get a little bit more sleep at night. Other simple things—showing patients how they can eat flavorful meals while restricting the salt in their diet, allowing them to drive again, encouraging them to begin some low-level exercise—are also important in improving quality of life.

Finally, let me say that this whole issue of quality of life, despite the development of better tools to measure it, remains extremely complex. Certainly, the quality of life of the patient who suffers with heart failure needs to be addressed, but I think in a broader sense quality of life refers to the patient in the context of family and friends. For example, I have one patient who seems to be honest when he says that he feels his quality of life has improved and that he feels well most of the time these days. Unfortunately, when I talk to the members of his family, who are so doting and meticulous in caring for him, I get the idea that although the patient feels well, the quality of life for his family has not improved! In fact, I think that their quality of life is worse because of all the things we have taught them to pay attention to. I think this all comes down to a need for having good communication among the patient, the family, the doctor, and the doctor's staff—communication in all directions, which sometimes involves very specific open-ended discussions about what is important to the patient and to the family and how to find a happy medium for everyone. I remember one near battle in my office when a patient came in with his wife. I had only met the wife on a couple of occasions, and she had very little to say. At the end of our visit the patient said to me, "Doc, please tell her that I can have some cheese." When this man first became my patient, my staff and I examined his eating habits and found that he was eating a great deal of salt in his food. We told him to limit certain high-salt foods like cheese, which he tried to do. A few weeks later he reported, "Doc, I've really cut down on virtually everything, but the one thing I really *must* have is some cheese." From the passion in this man's eyes it was clear that allowing him to eat a little cheese on a rare occasion would make his quality of life better and the rest of his low-salt diet much more palatable. The problem, however, was that his wife, who had never heard me relax my taboo against cheese, felt that she needed to be the self-appointed "salt police" for the patient. Husband and wife battled back and forth until I intervened. I tried to make clear to the wife how much I appreciated her efforts, how I wished that she could be in the home of many of my other patients who needed to be reminded to stick to their diet, and, finally, how I was reducing the severity of my injunction against cheese in her husband's case and allowing him to have a little at his own discretion. Although the issue surrounding food would seem to be a minor one, in this family, at least, this simple solution seemed to make a great deal of difference in determining the quality of life in the long run not only for this gentleman but for his entire family.

Improving the quality of life is an extremely important ingredient in the entire treatment regimen for patients with heart failure. I emphasize again the importance of communicating this issue to the physician because almost always some happy medium can be worked out to help improve the quality of life for patients and their families.

Chapter 14

How to Stay Out of the Hospital

I thought I would write this chapter because no matter what stage people with heart failure are in, everyone wants to stay out of the hospital. A lot of people first find out about their heart failure when they are initially admitted to a hospital, and of course any further admissions to the hospital represent a lack of progress, a sign of illness, and a step backward. It is common to have multiple admissions, and as the heart failure progresses, the time away from the hospital frequently becomes shorter and shorter. Perhaps you're one of those people who are told they have heart failure in their doctor's office, and you've not yet been hospitalized. Staying out of the hospital is one of your primary goals—and indeed it should be. Or you may be a family member for whom the hospitalization of a loved one is causing difficulty—the emotional pain in seeing your relative hospitalized, the inconvenience for you in getting back and forth to the hospital, the need to rearrange schedules, and the disruption of your everyday routine. There are many more reasons why we don't like to see patients with heart failure hospitalized, including the large economic burden, the time away from work, and the sense of illness that hospitals provide.

You may be a hospital administrator or a politician concerned with rising health care costs who realizes that for people over the age of 65 heart failure is the number one cause of admissions to all hospitals across our country. From an administrator's point of view, you are aware that with every hospitalization for a senior citizen with heart failure, you lose money. For example, currently Medicare reimburses a hospital just a little over $3,000 for every heart failure admission to the hospital and expects a length of stay in the hospital of no more than 5–6 days. However, the facts are that the average length of stay for a heart failure admission is almost 9 days and the cost is well over $10,000. If you were in business and losing approximately $7,000 on your number one sales item, you would be broke in no time.

It is clear that staying out of the hospital once you have heart failure is a measure of success. It represents the success of your treatment, it represents your ability to control your heart failure symptoms and progression by limiting your fluid and your salt, and in many respects it reflects the success in communication between you, your family, and your physician and other heart failure professionals. Hopefully, when you are in the hospital, a major "tune-up" will be performed so that all the extra fluid retained in your body and causing the swelling in your legs and in your liver, the fluid in your lungs, and so on, is removed and you get down to your dry weight. Also, you will have the opportunity to review the importance of fluid and salt restriction with one of the nurses, the doctor, or the dietitian. New medications may be prescribed, and you will have a chance to become familiar with their effects and regimen. Perhaps an exercise program will be discussed with you during that hospital period, or perhaps new support systems will be established for you as you talk with other heart failure patients, learn about support groups, or arrange to have visiting home health services after your discharge.

Steps to Take after Discharge

Whatever steps are taken in the hospital, it is imperative that you maximize those steps once you become an outpatient. What I would like to do in this chapter is list some of the important steps that you should take immediately upon being discharged from the hospital in order to prevent another admission. If you have never been hospitalized, these are steps that may help prevent an admission.

Check Your Weight

Surprisingly, body weight is one of the most informative and most accurate measurements doctors and nurses use to help monitor patients with heart failure. In the hospital, patients get weighed on a daily basis primarily to see if the extra fluid is coming off at a proper rate. Yes, there are other ways to assess fluid retention—by examining the legs, listening to the lungs, monitoring what doctors and nurses call "I and O," or fluid intake and output—but measuring a patient's weight is really a simple procedure that is reproducible from day to day.

Therefore, one of the most important pieces of medical equipment you can have in your home is a good scale. You do not need to purchase an expensive doctor's-office-type scale; any scale, whether it be digital or spring, will do. The main idea is to get into the habit of taking your weight each day at the same time with the same amount of clothing on.

Many patients weigh themselves first thing in the morning. You should probably urinate first and then weigh yourself; do this either before or after your bath or shower but preferably before you eat your breakfast and with approximately the same amount of clothing on (or even in the nude). At least for the first few weeks, or until you are well in the habit of noting it each day, you should write your weight down on a piece of paper. A written record, which shows the trend in your weight over a period of time, will be helpful when you call your doctor or when you go for an office visit.

Our nurses are always catching patients who have been told to weigh themselves but don't. Invariably, a patient will call and report being a little bit more short of breath since an office visit 3 weeks earlier. The nurse's first question will be, "Well, what is your weight today?" so that it can be compared to the weight 3 weeks ago. Patients who weigh themselves regularly can provide that piece of information immediately and precisely whereas those who have been skipping their daily chore of checking their weight will usually say "Oh, it's about the same" or "It's up just a little" or "I've noticed my clothes are a little bit tighter." But that kind of subjective measurement just won't do. You need to check your weight on a daily basis.

Monitor Your Fluid Intake and Your Urinary Output

Measurements of fluid intake and output are used in the hospital to make sure that a limited amount of fluid goes into the heart failure patient each day and that a sufficient amount of urine is being produced each day. When we are trying to get fluid off a patient, we want the output to exceed the intake. Once there is a period of stability, the intake and output n.ore closely coincide, though usually the output still exceeds the input by a slight amount. That is because in addition to the fluids taken in the body produces water as part of its natural metabolism.

Monitoring your intake at home is a fairly simple job. There are a variety of techniques people have used, but none is as simple as filling a $1\frac{1}{2}$ quart container with water and pouring an equivalent amount of this water out every time you take some liquid to drink. When the container is empty, you are done with your fluids for the day. This is a particularly good thing to do in the first weeks after you get home from the hospital, until you can accurately gauge exactly how much fluid is included in your fluid restriction. People often say, "Oh, Doc, I'm not drinking that much" or "I really don't take in that much pop or juice or milk each day," but once they start to keep track, they find out that they are in fact consuming a great deal of fluid.

The same sort of idea applies to output. Many people take home from the hospital the measuring cups or urinals they used there to keep track of their daily urinary output. This can be a little harder to do than it was during the hospital stay, particularly if a person is active and is spending a great deal of time away from home. That's why measuring the weight is the simplest and most efficient way to keep track of the fluid status of your body. However, many patients do keep quite accurate track of their urinary output, and I have had more than one patient report daily urine output to me with an accuracy of one cubic centimeter. Again, once there has been a period of stability and you are familiar with how much urine output you're having on a daily basis, you do not have to keep track of this as much, unless instructed to do so by your doctor.

After a few weeks of measuring output, people are actually quite good at estimating how much urine they are producing on a daily basis and can quickly tell you if their urinary output has dropped slightly, which is often one of the first signs that fluid retention is going on and that an oral diuretic has lost its effect. You should be aware that one of the common reasons for people with heart failure ending up back in the hospital is indiscretion in dietary habits, particularly in fluid or salt intake. Therefore, monitoring these "I's and O's" is really quite important.

Monitoring Your Sodium Intake

Since indiscretion in the diet is a common reason for another bout of heart failure, we urge people to become familiar with the total sodium contained in a 2,000-milligram sodium chloride diet, although most people use avoidance of salt as the basic way to monitor their sodium restriction. However, many patients do keep accurate records of their sodium intake and can tell you how many grams of salt they consume each day.

Quite often it is the spouse of the heart failure patient who keeps track of, and close control over, the sodium intake. I recall one patient in particular who came to see me after hospitalization for heart failure. His wife brought in some of the most meticulous records I have ever seen. They included every cubic centimeter of fluid taken in and every drop of urine put out. In fact, every morsel of food that went into this gentleman's body had a sodium content estimated and entered into a large handbook the couple carried around with them. The sections were color coded and divided into three periods of the day—overall, a splendid piece of work. For a short time the gentleman did well, and then I began to notice some fluid accumulation. A quick check of the records showed that something was amiss. After I spoke to the husband alone, I learned that he considered his wife to be so meticulous and so controlling in monitoring him that as a form of rebellion he was managing to sneak by the local hot dog stand on a daily basis.

The point here is that you really do need to restrict your intake of fluid and salt but that conscientious behavior is usually well reflected in your body weight; close counts of salt and fluid intake are primarily for educational purposes, that is, to train you to recognize what a proper heart failure diet is.

Know Your Medicines and Have an Ample Supply

Commonly, during a hospital visit for heart failure various new medicines are started and those a patient has been on for a long time are adjusted. One of my pet peeves is that most of the discharge planning, or preparation of the patient to go home from the hospital, takes place about 5 minutes before the patient walks out the door. It usually takes place right in the middle of the period when the nurse is terribly busy with other patients. The fact that the patient is eager to get out of the hospital and a family member has just come on a lunch break and is eager to get the patient home provides an added sense of pressure and urgency. Usually, patients are given some scrap of paper with so-called discharge instructions and sent on their merry way.

Ideally, the discharge planning process should start when the person is first admitted to the hospital. During hospitalization new medications patients are receiving should be explained and shown to them so that they can begin to recognize the form of the medication. We strongly recommend and try to use a medication chart that not only lists each medication along with the dose being prescribed but also indicates what the medication is for and at what time it should be taken. Therefore, to further your goal of staying out of the hospital, you need to know exactly what your medications are and precisely when to take them. There are many other things you need to know about your medications, such as whether they should be taken with food or without, whether they should be taken with other medicines or not, and what you should do if you miss a dose by an hour or so (some medications should be taken anyway, and others should be avoided because they would come too close to the next dose). These are questions that should be addressed to your doctor or nurse, but sometimes a pharmacist can give plenty of good information.

Another point I'd like to make is that patients should, whenever possible, become totally familiar with their medications and even carry a medication list with them at all times. I have seen a wide variety of these, from computer-generated printouts to handwritten lists, but they all work as long as the patients themselves know their medications. Many patients have their spouse or caregiver or home health nurse prepare their medications. This can often be a disaster because if that person is unavailable, some patients no longer know which medications to take and a few simple medication errors can land them right back in the hospital. You will also notice that when you go to your doctor's office for a visit, he or she may change medications based on your progress; you should have a way of quickly and clearly updating your medication list so that when you arrive home from the doctor's office there will be no confusion about exactly what changes were made.

Just as bad as not knowing your medicines or not knowing when to take them is running out of them. A large percentage of the phone calls doctors get on weekends are for prescription refills. When I see a patient in the office one of the last questions I almost always ask is, "Do you have enough of your medicines?" Many people do know, but it's surprising how many are not aware of the supply they have on hand. In fact, we are seeing more problems with this as more and more people are using mail-in prescription services. These services usually supply a 1-month or a 3-month supply of medication at one time. However, if at the end of 1 month we double the dose of a certain medication, a person will run out of that medication before the next prescription is due to be mailed to them. Therefore, it is always a good idea to check the medicines to make sure you have an ample supply. If there is ever a question about whether you are going to continue on a certain medication—that is, if your doctor has indicated to you that he or she might be eliminating a particular drug in the future or changing to a different formulation—check with your doctor's office before you refill that prescription; I hate to see a person buy a fresh supply of an expensive medication just before I discontinue prescribing it.

Know How Much Activity Is Expected of You

A great deal of confusion arises regarding how much activity patients should have once they go home from the hospital. I believe doctors always expect that patients will be more active at home, yet it is common for patients and family members to believe that patients should maintain the same activity level they had in the hospital. Lack of communication on this point frequently leads to patients remaining quite inactive at home, which is a problem not only because it results in a deconditioning of their muscles but also because it takes away one of the important tools doctors have in assessing how patients are progressing. For example, if you limit yourself to staying indoors and walking from room to room, your activity is so little that your doctor does not know how much activity you are really capable of.

You should ask, and your doctor should tell you, exactly what activities you may pursue once you leave the hospital (or once you are diagnosed). If this was not mentioned at the outset and you are limiting your activity to the point where you feel you could certainly do a great deal more, do not hesitate to call and discuss this with your doctor; he or she may not realize how limited your activity is. I recall seeing a particular patient intermittently for a couple of months as an outpatient. She was doing fairly well, and I wanted to cut back on some of the treatments she was getting. I asked her if she got out of breath when she exerted herself, and she replied no. I asked her if she got fatigued with her daily activities, and again she replied no. It was not until I specifically asked her what her daily activities were that she replied, "Well, doctor, you know that I never take more than twenty steps at a time." She then proceeded to explain to me that 2 years earlier, when she left the hospital after becoming ill for the first time, her doctor at the time told her never to take more than 20 steps at any one time. She had followed these instructions to a tee and for the subsequent 2 years had severely limited her activity.

You should get a clear picture about what your level of activity is and what you can and cannot do. I commonly tell patients to progressively do more and to try things. I tell them that when they get tired or feel exhausted or get out of breath, these are simply the ways the body uses to tell them that they've reached their limit for the moment. I encourage them to go back and try the same activity the next day or the day after to see if they can't do it a bit better or a little longer. Also, I often tell patients to do what they can or to gradually begin a very slow walking program at least until I see them in the office and perform a cardiopulmonary exercise test. Once I do that exercise test, I can frequently tell a patient more precisely what he or she should be doing and at what heart rate and, in fact, whether more exercise is going to help or hurt.

Keep an Accurate Assessment of Your Symptoms

Dr. Bernie Siegel has written another wonderful book, entitled *How to Live Between Office Visits*. While this is primarily a book regarding patient empowerment, faith, belief, and emotions, the practical question for the heart failure patient still remains: What should you do between office visits? Obviously, if there is a marked worsening of your symptoms after you leave the hospital or doctor's office, this is something you need to call your doctor about. However, you also need to keep track of minor changes, the day-to-day changes that are so important in helping your doctor guide your progress. For example, I frequently tell patients that I am changing their medication but want them to pay particular attention to what their energy level is like by noting such things as whether they are able to make their bed in the morning with less effort, whether they take fewer naps during the day, and whether they feel less fatigued at the end of the day. It is this sensitivity to changes in your body and in the way you feel that is so important in monitoring your progress. And, by the same token, in monitoring any changes in the other direction. Feeling more fatigued during the day, taking more naps, having more difficulty sleeping, discovering that doing a chore you've been used to doing on a regular basis is now more difficult—any of these can be a very early sign that you need more help for your heart failure.

In fact, it is usually these very early and subtle changes (like being able to walk up a flight of stairs without having to stop in the middle or at the top) that indicate when the medicines are finally kicking in and progress is being made. Therefore, you can help keep yourself out of the hospital by keeping accurate track of these common day-to-day activities. You should also know when to call your doctor. You will usually be given some guidelines; you may be instructed to call if, for example, your weight goes up by a certain amount, if you experience more shortness of breath, if you notice more swelling in your legs, if you have more difficulty breathing, and so on. If there is ever a question as to whether or not you should call your doctor, you probably should call. If you feel uncomfortable about a certain situation or feeling, a quick call is usually easier to deal with and will be more satisfying to both you and your doctor than an emergency hospital visit at 2 in the morning.

Having a practice that is dedicated exclusively to taking care of very sick patients with heart failure, I am honestly amazed at how few of my patients end up in the emergency room or being hospitalized or even how few calls I get on the weekend. I attribute this mostly to the wonderful education the patients get from the nurses but also to the encouragement we give our patients to call during the week to try to clarify little problems before they become big ones. Therefore, good communication is one of the factors will keep you out of the hospital.

Do All Those Little Things You Learned in the Hospital

Do the little things you learned during your hospital stay, even if you think they're not important and even if you don't like doing them because they remind you of being hospitalized. For example, when people come into the hospital with swollen legs, I usually order a pair of the thigh-high support hose and have the nurses help the patient put them on each morning and take them off at bedtime. These are yours, but most people take that souvenir of the hospital and neatly pack it away in one of their drawers. I encourage patients to use these stockings, particularly when their legs are swollen, but even when there is no swelling, the stockings provide a good deal of support and help the blood flow return in the legs. The legs of heart failure patients are clearly not normal and have altered patterns of blood flow return. If they are prescribed for you, you should try and use these stockings. You may have been given a lot of literature regarding heart failure in the hospital or in the doctor's office; you should review this information periodically and see if you can't learn one more thing about your heart failure each time you read through the materials.

If you can find out about a heart failure support group in your area, or you've been contacted by the Mended Hearts or some other support service, try to get involved. I think this gives patients a good frame of reference, allowing them to see what other patients do under similar circumstances, to compare notes, and to feel more like a member of a community and less like an isolated person with a disease.

Use Your Home Health Services

Many people go home from the hospital with some home nursing personnel, including visiting nurses, physical therapists, home health aides, and homemakers. You should know precisely who these people are and what their functions are when they come to your home. Also, you should know which doctor ordered their services and to whom they are reporting. You can use them as a liaison for many of your questions, although my experience has been that while they generally provide good general nursing care, most home care companies do not provide very specific information for heart failure patients. That is changing, however, and there are some specialized companies now emerging that are dedicated to providing general cardiac services and are quite knowledgeable about heart failure care.

If a physical therapist comes to your home, your job is to work hard with that therapist for the duration of the visit, not to entertain the person socially. The same thing is true for the home health nurse. While these people are usually kind and compassionate, their job is to find out how you are doing, and your job is to find out what other information you need to know about your heart failure. You need to use these professionals for the resources they are. They can also be important stopgaps to help you avoid returning to the hospital. If you are experiencing symptoms—more shortness of breath, more leg swelling, an increase in weight—you may be able to get a home health nurse to come to your home that evening or the next day with instructions from the doctor before you would be able to reach the doctor yourself. Also, the nurse might be better able to assess your symptoms than you are and can help you decide whether you need to go to the emergency room or whether you can wait to contact a doctor the following morning.

Educate Yourself

Once you are home from the hospital, you should, besides doing all the things your doctors and nurses ask you to do, take it upon yourself to find out more about your condition and what can be done for it. This includes not only going to the library to read some general information about heart disease but also perhaps visiting a medical library, getting information from your local heart association, and keeping your eyes and ears open for radio and TV broadcasts about advances in the treatment of heart failure. I am not surprised when we get half a dozen phone calls the day after a news broadcast about some advance in the treatment of heart failure, all inquiring about that new technique or new investigational drug. What actually does surprise me is that we only receive half a dozen calls. Extrapolating from my experience, I conclude that of the thousands and thousands of people who heard that announcement, most have not yet begun to take full charge and control of their disease. While it can be argued that in the hospital patients lose a lot of their privacy and power—and although there are many ways to combat this, the truth is that the hospital environment is far from ideal, from both the physician's and the patient's standpoint—once they are out of the hospital and become their own person again it is their duty to regain their empowerment and take control of their disease. In other words, at that point the professionals are not the patients' masters or leaders but simply their guides.

It is in the week or so after hospitalization that you should reread the materials you were given, rethink the things you were told, and try to make a sensible plan that fits with your lifestyle and your goals. If things do not fit, discussing them with your doctor at the next visit is probably one of the most important parts of that visit.

I believe the steps outlined here will be helpful to you as you try to plan your own course of therapy after you've left the hospital (and will certainly help you avoid an initial hospitalization). I think they focus on areas in which you can take control and in many ways be the master of your fate, in terms of preventing a hospital visit.

The wife of one of my patients said to me recently that she and her husband felt there were not many positive things going on in his life. He had to watch his fluid and salt intake, but only the exercise I recommended for him felt to him like something he could be in control of. I feel that all the steps I've presented so far in this chapter— watching fluid intake, watching salt consumption, exercising, taking your daily weight—are things that you can actively become involved in and that can really make a significant difference in the overall progress and outcome of your heart failure.

How to Visit Your Doctor

The next step after you have been out of the hospital is planning for your next (or your initial) outpatient visit with your doctor. Often patients don't know what to bring with them to the visit in terms of records, and I thought I would suggest a few things that might make your visit more efficient and more informative.

If you have been keeping accurate track of your daily weights (as you should) and have monitored your intake and output, bring those records with you. What happens to your weight in your first 2 or 3 days at home is often much more important to me than the difference between your weight at the hospital before you left and your weight in my office on the day of your visit; your home scale will be the most consistent over those initial few days.

You should also bring with you all of your medication bottles as well as your list of medications. At your first visit the doctor or nurses will check that the prescriptions you actually got filled are exactly what the doctor wants you to be taking. Yes, it is possible for doctors to make errors in writing prescriptions and for pharmacists to make errors in filling them. So on the first hospital discharge visit I make sure that the medication list is accurate and that the identity and dosage of pills the patient has reflect what I think they are taking. You should also bring with you any other medicines the doctor may not know you are taking, including vitamins, minerals, or over-the-counter medications. While you may think these medications are safe, they may have important interactions with the drugs you are taking, and bringing them in gives the doctor a good opportunity to review that possibility with you. You should also be prepared to tell the doctor what activities you have been engaging in since you left the hospital. I always find helpful the remarks patients make regarding what they think they are able to do, whether they get more or less winded than before, and whether they feel more or less fatigued after a particular activity. I also ask patients what they do on a daily basis. If they have not thought about this or have not written down a few notes, they usually can't tell me what their activities have been. I am particularly interested in what they are able to do when they leave the house, for example, if they are able to walk around the mall, visit their children, or go out for dinner with friends and family. At this office visit I welcome questions regarding fluid and salt restriction, and while we do not solicit them, it is surprising how often we get true confessions about failing to stick to the dietary restrictions, along with fervent promises to reform.

You should bring with you at every office visit a list of questions you have regarding your condition and treatment. Now not every health care question needs to be addressed to or is appropriate for the doctor who treats your heart failure. For example, when patients come to see me for their heart failure and they have another primary care doctor, I'm usually not the one to answer questions about their diabetes, although I will inquire about it. Also, if they have another medical problem unrelated to their heart failure, I usually will refer that to their primary care physician. Often, however, patients don't know which doctor they should be addressing which questions to, and it is fair game to bring them up.

The questions patients often ask at the first office visit have to do with their recent hospitalization; most want to know the nature and meaning of the results of all the testing that was done in the hospital. They might also begin to ask questions about what the alternatives for therapy are and what the plans are for their short-, medium-, and long-term care. Commonly, questions come up regarding their ability to drive again or to travel. I often feel that patients and their families believe the cardiologist is the only person capable of deciding when the patient can drive. Now for those who have severe irregularities of the heartbeat, the answer is clear: Patients who have suffered a sudden passing out because of the irregularity of their heartbeats or who have implanted defibrillators should not drive. However, many people with heart failure do not have these problems, and the question always arises (usually from adult children concerned about a parent) as to whether or not they are capable of driving. Patients often reason that since they have been driving safely for many years, they can continue to do so. They usually add that they are not going to go far, only within the neighborhood. At this point one of my nurses always hastens to add the fact that most accidents occur within a mile of home.

The concern of family members is for the safety of the patient, of the passengers in the patient's car, and indeed of community members at large. Often the concern extends beyond this to questions of liability and insurance coverage. I almost always feel that I am about to enter a family battle when I ask at the end of the office visit of a senior patient if there are any questions and the son or daughter says, "Go ahead, Dad, ask him. Ask him if you can drive." The senior citizen then sheepishly asks about getting behind the wheel again, and everyone stares at me for the final word on whether or not the patient can safely drive. The truth of the matter is that I really don't know most of the time. I base my opinion on whether the person has been stable, whether laboratory tests show no major fluctuations, and whether there seems to be no susceptibility for sudden cardiac death. However, I think the issue is by and large one of liability, and I am usually reluctant to pronounce a level of safety for anyone to drive. I think this question should be resolved within the family after getting an opinion from the cardiologist or family doctor, but the final opinion does not and should not rest with the doctors.

Also at the office visit you should mention any medication you seem to be running low on and may run out of before the next office visit. In fact, you should ask when that office visit might be, and if the interval seems either too short or too long, you should inquire as to the reasoning. Use this visit to begin to get comfortable with your doctor, particularly if he or she is new to you. You might want to ask such specific questions as the following: "When is a good time for me to make a phone call to your office?"; "What is the best way to get a prescription refilled?"; "What should I do if there is an emergency?"; "Should I go to the closest hospital, or should I try to get to the hospital where you are on staff?"

Many of my colleagues bristle at the idea of being called by their first name. I think at some point you ought to determine your doctor's preference about this—as well as reveal to him or her your preference on how you would like to be addressed. Remember that this is probably going to be a long-standing relationship between you and your doctor. Personally, I try to gauge what form of address my patients are comfortable with, and often I ask them. I think that doctors and nurses far too often assume a first-name intimacy and that this makes many patients, particularly the elderly, uncomfortable. On the other hand, using first names provides a sense of comfort for many patients and breaks down barriers. It's simply a matter of exercising good communication skills for doctors to inquire about this or to get a sense of it early on in a relationship. Patients have a similar responsibility. I have patients who call me by my first name; in fact, I think many of them do it as a sort of a test, to see what my reaction will be. Sometimes I detect other reasons. For example, the other day a patient I saw two or three times, a gentleman who really has not been making much progress with his heart failure, suddenly addressed me by my first name. I immediately sensed that this was not an attempt to try to develop more of a friendship but an expression of his frustration with his lack of progress. I stopped the routine inquiries regarding his heart failure, looked at him, and asked, "What really seems to be bothering you the most?" He broke down and told me that he was concerned that he was probably going to die soon since there was currently nothing that I could do for him. I told him that I had been trying to manage him quite conservatively because of his many associated medical conditions. It was at that point that he opened up and said, "Doc, I don't care what you have to do, but I've got to feel better than I do now or life is not worth living." We subsequently tried a more aggressive approach in his treatment, and fortunately it worked. Soon thereafter I noticed that he was addressing me as Doctor Silver again. I mentioned this to him, he apologized for having called me by my first name, we had a long talk about our preferences, and I believe we arrived at an agreement that both of us feel comfortable with. The point is, the "correct" names for the doctor and the patient are the ones they are comfortable with. As always, nothing compares with good communication and discussion.

As you can see, there really are many issues that need to be addressed at each office visit. In the treatment of heart failure patients, a visit often results in changes in therapy or a reevaluation of the treatment strategy, which elicit a new and longer list of questions from the patient at the following visit. Perhaps that is why I enjoy treating patients with heart failure so much. There is really very little status quo. Patients do not stay stable for months or years at a time; they are either getting better or getting worse. I enjoy the challenge of getting everyone to make progress and move forward.

I think you can use the suggestions made in this chapter to take control over some aspect of your heart failure, to gain a better understanding of your treatments and your doctor's plans for you, and to help ensure that you stay out of the hospital and make the best use of your outpatient visits.

Chapter 15

The Young Person with Heart Failure

The majority of patients in this country who have heart failure are over the age of 65. That is not to say, however, that the younger patient is immune to serious heart disease or heart failure. The comments in this book apply to heart failure patients of any age. There are, however, special forms of heart failure that the younger patient may have:

1. Cardiomyopathy due to congenital heart disease
2. Alcohol-induced cardiomyopathy
3. Dilated cardiomyopathy with or without myocarditis
4. Diabetic cardiomyopathy
5. Familial cardiomyopathy
6. Chemotherapy-related cardiomyopathy
7. Cardiomyopathy due to premature coronary artery disease (heart attacks) or severe hypertension
8. AIDS-related cardiomyopathy
9. Peripartum cardiomyopathy

Obviously, these are, with the exception of peripartum cardiomyopathy, forms of heart failure that can develop in people at any age, but some of these distinct forms tend to occur in younger patients. For example, while diabetic cardiomyopathy can certainly occur in any individual who has diabetes, studies have shown that diabetics on insulin, compared to nondiabetics, have a 2.4-fold higher incidence of developing heart failure and that this generally occurs at a younger age. Similarly, alcohol-related cardiomyopathy can occur at any age, but the patient with the new onset of heart failure who has an abuse pattern of alcohol related to it is frequently a 20-, 30-, or 40-year-old.

In a moment I will discuss some of the specific forms, but there are some interesting statistics surrounding the younger patient with heart failure. It has long been known that older age gives a worse prognosis for patients with heart failure, but I am not convinced that younger age generally connotes a better prognosis. For example, according to one of the large heart failure data bases (Studies on Left Ventricular Dysfunction [SOLVD] Registry), patients older than the age of 76 have a greater than 38% 1-year mortality rate. Patients aged 21 to 55, however, have only a 16.6% mortality rate for the same 1-year period. These statistics reflect a shorter period or duration of heart failure in the younger individuals or less serious disease. Since many younger individuals tend to get forms of heart failure that are reversible, the statistics reflect the greater likelihood of spontaneous remission or attenuation in these patients. For example, a young person with an undiagnosed case of myocarditis may have rather severe heart failure within the first year, but the condition may progressively improve or stabilize, and a large percentage of young women with peripartum cardiomyopathy, which I will discuss shortly, return completely to normal function. Moreover, while I mentioned earlier that there is a major increase in death from heart failure in this country, one of the few groups in which there has been a decline is white patients under the age of 45. The exact reasons for this decline and for the racial differences in susceptibility of this age group are unclear at the present time.

When I see young persons with severe heart failure, I always think of the many productive years they should have ahead of them and I redouble my efforts to find a reversible cause for their heart failure and to seek therapies that will not only make a major functional improvement in their lifestyle and quality of life but prolong their life.

Common Pathways to Heart Failure in the Young

Young patients who have heart failure develop it from one of four common pathways. A young patient may have congenital heart disease, or a heart defect from birth; both individuals whose heart defect was surgically repaired and those whose defect was never detected may have heart damage, with long-term malfunction of the heart muscle leading to heart failure.

Another very common situation is the development of a form of dilated cardiomyopathy (weak heart muscle). For example, young people may have bouts of myocarditis, or inflammation of the heart muscle, which may ultimately lead to a dilated cardiomyopathy. Or they may develop a spontaneous case of dilated cardiomyopathy, which we see all too frequently. According to some studies, up to 80% of all new cases of heart failure in young patients are due to idiopathic dilated cardiomyopathy, which means the exact cause is unknown. A dilated cardiomyopathy in young patients is often directly related to alcohol abuse. Alcohol is a direct toxin (or damaging substance) to the heart muscle. Excessive alcohol can cause a severe weakness of the heart, but, with early cessation, the heart muscle function often returns to normal. As the abuse continues for longer periods of time, however, the damage becomes irreversible. I often see young men and women who drink more than a case of beer each weekend and then wonder why they have developed heart disease. This is an important, and potentially preventable, form of heart failure.

There is also a rare form of dilated cardiomyopathy that seems to be familial (that is, it runs in families) and frequently affects young patients. Often in these familial cases there is some specific defect, such as an abnormality in the mitochondria (tiny powerplants in all our cells which create the energy necessary to perform work) or a genetic deficiency in a substance such as carnitine (a substance the body uses to help burn fatty acids or fats as fuel for the muscles).

Unfortunately, despite educational efforts regarding the need to control blood pressure, stop smoking, and reduce cholesterol in the diet, we still see many young people who have very advanced forms of coronary artery disease and who even develop heart attacks. In the past, when I saw a 40-year-old with new heart failure, I would rarely consider doing an angiogram to see if there was coronary artery disease, but in the last 5 or 6 years I've encountered severe coronary disease in young patients in their twenties and thirties often enough that I now frequently consider the possibility of a heart attack even in this age group. Although some of these patients have familiar forms of high levels of cholesterol and have very specific forms of coronary artery disease, others have simply engaged in self-abusive behavior, like smoking cigarettes and maintaining a high-fat diet, starting at a young age. So the young person who has suffered one or more heart attacks is certainly susceptible to developing heart failure.

Finally, one of the more unfortunate forms of heart failure that develops in a young person is what we call peripartum cardiomyopathy. For some as yet unknown reason some young women either during their last 3 months of pregnancy or within the first 3 months after delivery are susceptible to developing what we call a peripartum cardiomyopathy, whose exact cause has not yet been determined. Because the disease tends to appear in somewhat less affluent populations, nutritional deficiency has been suggested as the cause. Other suggested causes include toxemia, very high blood pressure developing during pregnancy, antibodies (the immune system of the body attacking itself), an allergic reaction to certain drugs, and genetic susceptibility. Black women have a higher incidence of peripartum cardiomyopathy than white women, and advanced maternal age, numerous past pregnancies, and twin pregnancies seem to predispose women to this disease. However, I would like to emphasize that there really is no way to predict who might develop this disease; in my own personal experience I have seen a preponderance of women who are white, pregnant for the first time, with a single baby, and with none of the other predisposing factors just mentioned. Inflammation of the heart muscle, or myocarditis, is commonly suspected as the cause of this form of cardiomyopathy. In one study, 14 of 18 women who had this cardiomyopathy were shown to have myocarditis on a biopsy of the heart muscle. Often, however, we find no cause whatsoever. The bad news is that this can be a very serious form of cardiomyopathy, in fact, it can be fatal. On the other hand, many women do recover.

From various studies and my own personal experience, I would say that there is complete recovery in one-third of women with this disease, with one-third stabilizing and one-third dying from it. In the latter there is often overwhelming myocarditis. While we frequently try to discourage subsequent pregnancies in women who have had this disease, with very careful testing we can determine which women can go on and deliver babies in the future without any difficulty. We do know that a woman who has had a peripartum cardiomyopathy is at very high risk for worsening heart failure with subsequent pregnancies. However, because of their young age many of these women do want to consider additional pregnancies. In that case, I usually recommend a minimum period of 2 years from the time of the cardiomyopathy to allow for an adequate period of stabilization and observation. During that time I watch the patient carefully to make sure she has no early symptomatic recurrence of her heart failure. If she is completely stable and asymptomatic over that period of time, I make several measurements, including either an echo or MUGA, to follow the overall function of the left ventricle. I also commonly rely on cardiopulmonary exercise testing to determine how the heart muscle may respond during pregnancy, which places a variety of stresses on even the normal heart. Since it is important to gauge how the extra blood volume and energy requirements of a pregnancy may affect a previously damaged heart muscle, the overall efficiency and ability to exercise adequately on the cardiopulmonary exercise test is one of the measurements I rely on before condoning a young woman's decision to become pregnant again after she has suffered peripartum cardiomyopathy.

Chemotherapy-Related Cardiomyopathy

Certain forms of chemotherapy, or drugs used to fight cancers, can cause serious heart muscle damage and heart failure. The risk for developing heart muscle damage seems to be related to the total dose of medication received (usually adriamycin), the combination of other heart-damaging chemotherapeutic agents, such as high dose cyclophosphamide, and radiation treatment for the tumor. This type of cardiomyopathy is commonly seen today in younger women who have undergone chemotherapy for breast cancer, but it is also commonly seen in patients who received these treatments for various forms of lymphoma. It is a very sad situation when a young patient who has licked one serious disease develops another because of the treatment received. Often this form of heart failure develops very suddenly; unfortunately, it is usually a progressive and eventually fatal form of heart failure. Cancer specialists and cardiologists are working closer together nowadays to better study the heart muscle after each round of chemotherapy in hopes of preventing heart failure due to the cancer treatment and to develop alternative therapies that can be given to people who are susceptible to this kind of damage. If you are getting chemotherapy with adriamycin, you may want to keep track of the total dose you have received because the overall risk of damage to the heart muscle increases greatly beyond a certain threshold. If you have had any prior cardiac history, including high blood pressure or prior heart attack, you may be more susceptible to the development of heart failure while undergoing treatment with anticancer drugs.

AIDS and Heart Failure

Finally, there is a great deal of media attention on the epidemic of AIDS, which continues to take approximately 50,000 lives annually in the United States. I am frequently asked about the relationship between AIDS, heart disease, and heart failure. AIDS tends to predominantly affect young people, and some of the very early research I did at the National Institutes of Health was on the cardiac involvement in young patients who died of AIDS. What we found initially was that Kaposi's sarcoma, a blood vessel tumor, occurs in patients with AIDS and affects the heart. Shortly thereafter, we found that there is also inflammation of the heart muscle, or a form of myocarditis, in these young patients. Today it is widely recognized that the heart is commonly involved in patients who have AIDS, and as often as 50% of the time myocarditis is found in the heart of an AIDS victim. Heart involvement can present in a variety of ways, including inflammation of the lining of the heart, fluid between the two layers of the heart, inflammation of the heart muscle, and even infection of the heart valves. Suffice it to say that heart failure is not uncommon in patients with AIDS and usually coexists with other forms of disability. Overall, it has been estimated that 2% to 10% of patients with AIDS will develop congestive heart failure related to their illness. There has not been any evidence that links the development of heart failure with how a patient contracted AIDS, but one study suggest that patients with lower counts of certain white blood cells, or infection-fighting cells, are most susceptible.

There are particular treatment dilemmas in treating patients with AIDS. One of the ways we try to treat inflammation in the heart muscle of patients in general is by suppressing the person's immune system. The patient with AIDS already has a suppressed immune system, and there are ongoing studies that are trying to determine if further immunosuppression is beneficial or detrimental. Also, some of the drug therapies used to treat AIDS patients may in fact cause a form of heart failure. It is this effect of the drug AZT that may limit its use in patients with AIDS.

Special Considerations with the Younger Patient

Regardless of what the cause of heart failure is in young patients, basically the same approach is applied to them in terms of trying to discover the cause and estimate the prognosis and of initiating the proper drug therapy and then fine-tuning the dosage. However, there are some very special considerations in the case of the young person, in contrast to the 75-year-old, who has heart failure. Probably one of the most obvious is that not only are we trying to achieve the goals mentioned in previous chapters regarding improved survival, functional improvement, and a better quality of life but we are also interested in sustaining all of these benefits over an extended period of time.

It is especially painful to see a young person with advanced heart failure, because we know that we may not be able to help him or her live into maturity. It is sometimes more difficult for me to approach young patients who have heart failure. Frequently, they must go from a stage in which they must accept the fact that they are temporarily sick and may be off work for a while to a stage in which they must face the fact that they have a life-threatening disease and that it is not only their years of livelihood that might be cut short but their life span as well. While I go out of my way to provide hope and help for these young patients in particular, I can honestly say that the loss of a young patient to heart failure is certainly one of the most painful experiences I go through. I think that this potential for premature death is one of the strongest motives in referring a patient to a transplant program rather quickly. As we have discussed earlier, however, the long waiting times for transplantation and the lack of donors limit transplantation as an option. Also we need to recall that transplantation may not be truly a permanent solution, in that it generally allows a 20-year-old to reach the ripe old age of 70 or 80, at least according to our current experience. Also, it involves many quality-of-life issues, especially for a younger patient. Fortunately, we are getting better at determining who might need a transplant; we now base our decisions on information provided by such testing as the cardiopulmonary exercise test rather than rely only on functional status or ejection fractions.

Another thing to consider for the young patient is the lifestyle that person leads. The 80-year-old, 70-year-old, or even 60-year-old may be able to retire or certainly will not have a daily requirement to get up and go to work. Retirement may not be possible for the younger patient with heart failure, which presents an additional worry and burden to the patient and family members. Frequently, the spouse has to find a job to maintain the family's lifestyle, and I've seen several young families undergo major changes because of this. The steps required to get financial assistance usually require using up all other family assets, and this only serves to further demoralize and break apart the family unit. The young person with heart failure certainly requires as much emotional and psychological support as does the elderly patient, perhaps even more, since the latter has had some time to adjust to a more limited lifestyle. It is also difficult to explain to children why their mother or father cannot be as active with them as they were before.

Because of the suddenness with which heart failure comes on in some young patients, there is frequently a period of disbelief, anger, and often even refusal to accept all the treatments that are necessary. With alcohol- or cocaine-related cardiomyopathy this reaction may be related to the substance abuse itself, but usually it is a reflection of the young person's sense of immortality. Great anguish accompanies the clash between this youthful sense of immortality and the harsh reality of personal mortality that must be faced by the young person with any serious disease, including heart failure. Fortunately, there are support groups available, such as Young Hearts, an organization founded in the Chicago area (see Appendix II), so that younger patients can discuss common issues with a group of peers. Since the issues facing younger and older patients differ, it is important to have support groups that focus on one or the other age group so that group members receive the specific emotional support and counseling needed for their form of heart disease.

Conclusion

Young persons with heart failure truly represent a very special situation. They are special in terms of the forms of heart failure they get as well as the socioeconomic problems that go with their heart failure. The aims and goals for treatment of these patients are also different. I must emphasize the importance of support and education for younger patients with heart failure. They may be at a stage in life when they have not yet started a family and may lack strong social support. They are often overwhelmed by fears of being sick and thoughts of mortality. I feel strongly that every effort should be made to find a reversible cause for heart failure in every patient, but this is especially so in the case of the younger patient. We must guide these patients to a better understanding of their disease so that they can seek treatment, accept help, and learn to lead active, productive lives despite often significant physical limitations. I believe that treating the younger patient with heart failure is one of the great challenges we must face.

Chapter 16

For Families Only

I remember one particular occasion when I first saw a new patient who was 80 years of age. She came to the office accompanied by two loving daughters and a son. We spent a great deal of time discussing her heart failure and the other treatments she had received. I told her quite honestly that there were many things we could try and that I felt there was great hope for some improvement in how she felt and in her ability to do more. You could see the light come on in this woman's face. I looked at her children, who were all nodding their heads in agreement and presenting courteous smiles on their faces, but when I got up to leave the room, they followed me out into the hallway. One of them said, "Doc, thanks so much for giving her that encouragement. It's nice to see her smile again," but then said, "Now, Doc, tell us what's really going to happen to Mom." I told them the same thing I tell every family member who follows me out into the hall or who calls me back the following day: I do not say anything to patients that I do not think is true. I honestly believe there is hope and help for almost everyone with heart failure.

Yes, there are patients for whom I feel nothing more

can be done. I usually tell them so quite honestly, although they often suspect it long before I tell them. I do not believe in either overinflating or hiding from a patient any of the realities of his or her prognosis. After all, these individuals are my patients, and it is to them that I must communicate the good and the bad but always the truth. The point is that most doctors are quite honest with their patients, and unless you suspect that a doctor is saying some things to your family member for moral support alone, I do not recommend that you follow the doctor out into the hall or corner him or her outside the hospital room and whisper about your family member. This only puts doubt in the mind of the patient. When family members approach me in this way, I frequently take them back into the room in front of the patient, readdress their concerns, and state once again that I do not say anything to the family that I wouldn't say directly to the patient. I think that family members can be very supportive of their sick relative by asking their questions and stating their concerns in the presence of the patient.

I think there are many other ways that families can be supportive of and extremely helpful to the patient with heart failure. These are ways in addition to helping patients shop, get their medications, visit the library to obtain more information about their heart problem, or write to the American Heart Association. One of the things I frequently tell my patients and their families to do is to discuss among themselves what they want done in the event of an emergency, that is, if the person has a cardiac arrest. Does the patient want to be resuscitated? Does he or she want to be on a ventilator? I also encourage patients and their families to discuss the concept of a living will. They usually don't make all of these decisions by themselves—I think that for many families and patients this is a pretty difficult experience—but at least this topic gets them going on the road to communicating with one another once again. I think it also serves to emphasize that heart failure is a very serious disease. Many families need to be made aware of this and need to learn to talk to one another again in loving and caring ways. Knowing that the ill family member may not be around within the next year or so can sometimes break down the anger that has unknowingly built up over the years. Trivial events in the past can now be overshadowed by current needs if families just let them. Families must bear the responsibility of being the patient's major source of support. It is not the responsibility of hospitals, other institutions, or doctors. The major source of support for the patient must come from the family.

One concept that Dr. Bernie Siegel makes perfectly clear in his writings is that people—patients and families —need to understand that death comes to everyone. And that death is not a failure. It is not a failure of the person who suffers with the disease, it is not a failure of the family, it is not a failure of the doctor, and it is not a failure of modern medicine. It is simply the inevitable failure of the body, and when everything has been done that can be done, people need to face death not as a failure of their ability to live but with rejoicing for the life they have had. Nor do I view as failures those patients who have severe heart failure because they ate too much fat and cholesterol, smoked too many cigarettes, or drank too much in their younger years. If they can control these habits now and take control over their disease by learning about their medications and educating themselves about fluid and salt restriction, then they in fact are successes. Who among us has done everything right all the time? We all make mistakes, and it is, more than anything else, the ability to communicate, to touch souls with one another, that makes us successful. And family members are in a position to make the greatest contribution to this communication.

While communicating early with a patient should be a two-way street, all too often it starts out as a one-way affair. Worse than that, nobody knows whose job it is to start the flow of communication. It would be wonderful if all patients who had heart failure could reach out and talk to their family and tell them what they were going through, but this is often very difficult to do. The reason I hear most often from my patients is that they don't want to burden their spouse, their son, their daughter, their grandchildren. And, therefore, the patient frequently remains silent. On the other hand, family members themselves are often reluctant to start communicating because they think the patient is weak, tired, or just not up to a long-winded conversation. Most important of all, many people suffer anxiety when faced with the need to confront the subject of death.

I remember treating a middle-aged woman who had been very active until she developed a serious form of heart failure. When she first came to see me, her two children were 18 and 20, and she still enjoyed picking out special Christmas presents for them. As her heart failure got worse and her energy level dropped, she found that she had less and less energy for her special shopping at Christmas time each year. At first she would pick out whatever she could find in a single store, and later she found herself just giving money to the children as presents. I could tell from her comments to me that she felt great pain in no longer being able to buy presents for her children. Furthermore, she was not able to have an open conversation with them and say, "Look, kids, I really am being affected by my illness. I love you just as much but simply can't get out to buy the presents any more. Do you understand?" On the other hand, her children, who probably didn't care what she got them for presents, were also unable to open up the conversation and say, "Look, Mom, we know that you are tired more and have less energy. It is not the Christmas presents that we're concerned about; we're just happy that you're here with us. What can we do to make life easier for you?"

Now every family's dynamics are different, but husbands and wives, fathers and sons, and mothers and daughters all have very special relationships to one another. I don't think that doctors or nurses—or even psychologists or psychiatrists—can have the impact on patients that family members can have simply by communicating with them. That is why I've written this chapter. I'd like to see one party or the other—patient or family—start the one-way communication and pursue it until it becomes a two-way street where conversation, laughter, and tears are going back and forth across it.

I mentioned earlier that whether or not a heart failure patient continues to drive is a decision that needs to be made by patients and their family and not really by the doctor. Yes, ask the doctor what he or she thinks about driving for the patient, but in the end it is going to have to be a family decision. Another decision that frequently has to be made concerns the patient's living accommodations. Frequently, elderly patients who have heart failure (or any disease, for that matter) need to make a change in their environment. Perhaps they need to find an apartment that is on the first floor because they cannot walk up the stairs any longer or need to move in with a son or daughter because they can't manage on their own. These kinds of decisions are tough at best but are almost always reached more easily when families can sit down together and discuss the pros and cons; under such circumstances a solution that is amenable to all is more likely to be hammered out. We do not need Henry Kissinger to come into our family kitchens and living rooms but simply a willingness to understand what the family member with heart failure is going through, what his or her needs are, and what we as family members can do to help.

Probably one of the most important ways I have seen families support patients with heart failure is by helping them set goals and priorities. Probably one of the hardest passages there is for young men and women who watch an elderly parent grow old, get sick, and approach death is to change roles in the parent–child relationship and assume the role of caretaker. Having to address questions regarding nursing homes, home care, and even funeral arrangements are important steps that patients and families can take together. The family can help by setting positive goals. One of the most remarkable patients I care for is a 93-year-old man whose wife is one of the most positive influences I have ever seen. She is fortunate to have her health but instead of bemoaning how ill her husband is and how limited he is, she continues to plan excursions, jaunts, and goals for him. Every time they come into the office she says something like, "Well, we just got back from our granddaughter's wedding in Iowa, and now we are planning to attend our grandson's birthday in Michigan." Every time they come in, she has a new goal for him. Continuing to establish short- and medium-term goals for patients with heart failure is, I think, one of the most important functions families can serve.

Finally, let me say that whether or not you think your family has strong emotional bonds, families are the basis of our emotional selves. So I urge families to get involved, to talk to their loved ones, to investigate what can be done for the member with heart failure, and to give that person a hug or simply express love and support for him or her. Family members need to help sick members not only make decisions regarding investigational trials and get their medicines but also take charge of their health through empowerment rather than allow others to treat them like a dependent child.

It is interesting that some of the strongest family support comes to patients who are the sickest with their heart failure. Now this probably does not surprise you, but I'll tell you why it surprises me. As I think about some of my sickest patients, I think that many of them are among the most fortunate. Despite their serious illness, they have tremendous support and understanding from their families. I am thinking of one woman in particular who has outlived virtually everyone's expectations for her, including my own. Now, this patient's family could simply coddle her and restrict her activities and be well justified in doing so. However, they have learned from both the patient and me that she is going to have good days and bad days with her illness. She also has an openness and willingness to communicate to her family when she is having a good day and when she is having a bad one. Both patient and family take full advantage of the good days, and I frequently hear not only about the days when my patient is sick and requires additional medication but also about the days when she is out in the shopping mall, even if she has to be pushed in a wheelchair. The point is that she is in control and, along with her family, makes the decisions from day to day.

Other patients who are not nearly as limited may have a family whose members simply concentrate on the heart failure. They prescribe their own brand of well-intentioned limitations, which only serve to demoralize and decondition the patient even more. They have not made a full effort to understand the disease their loved one has, and as a result they are doing them a disservice. I believe this approach is often adopted out of love for the sick member, but at the same time it reveals a fear of ongoing communication.

I am reminded of the story of the young man named Lorenzo Odone. You may have seen the wonderful movie called *Lorenzo's Oil*, which portrays the endless fight Lorenzo's mother and father put up in their effort to find a treatment for the rare nervous system disease he had. These parents loved their child, but what parent does not? The difference here is that these parents showed affection for their son by getting to know everything they could about his disease and struggling with him to find a cure.

In sum, family members can help a patient with heart failure enormously. They can help in obvious ways such as picking up medications, giving them a ride, or simply helping with the grocery shopping. I think, however, the most important way family members can help is by making sure the patient who suffers with heart failure does not suffer alone. Get to know about the disease and what can be done for it, and become a true partner for your family member who suffers. It is with that kind of communication and love that the suffering comes to an end and the healing truly begins.

Chapter 17

Future Possibilities and Probabilities

When I talk with my patients about some of the prognostic indicators with heart failure, I remind them that I do not have a crystal ball and cannot see what lies down the road for them. I tell them that we use the prognostic indicators as a guide to where they might be in the near future. I think looking at the future possibilities and probabilities for heart failure treatment is much the same. And if you asked 100 health professionals in this country about how heart failure will be treated in the next decade, you might well get 100 different answers. However, I'd like to highlight in this chapter what I think are some of the future trends in approaching heart failure at least over the next decade or so.

First and foremost, I think the medical approach to heart failure is going to be driven by a socioeconomic force sooner rather than later. Because of the ever-increasing number of patients with heart failure and the enormous economic burden to our health care system, as well as to the finances of individual families, heart failure is gaining a lot of attention at both national and local political levels. I believe heart failure will be one of the disease processes that will be targeted to require that physicians demonstrate that some of the treatments we currently use actually impact on outcomes. As applied to heart failure, "*outcome*" is a word with political and socioeconomic connotations that include not only all of the goals I mentioned before, including longevity, functional ability, and quality of life, but also the idea of the economic cost of caring for patients with heart failure. I think we should welcome this outcome-based approach as long as the initial goals are emphasized and everything is not reduced to a simple "bottom line."

For many years I have told other doctors that my opinion is that heart failure is an outpatient disease. Considering that the number one cause for hospitalization of patients over the age of 65 is heart failure, they find my statement hard to believe. However, as we move closer to adopting an outcome-driven approach to heart failure, we will increasingly find that more and more patients can be managed in an outpatient setting and that the number of hospital admissions for these patients will be markedly reduced. How this will happen is suggested in many of the chapters in this book.

In terms of diagnosis of heart failure, I think we will continue to emphasize the importance of finding the etiology accurately, since there will probably be better specific treatments for heart failure based on particular etiologies. I am certain that we will have better high-tech ways of sorting out the nonspecific diagnosis of dilated cardiomyopathy into more specific diagnoses that can be accurately assessed and treated. I think we will find better ways to diagnose myocarditis as well as familial forms of dilated cardiomyopathy, and in the not too distant future we'll probably use gene therapy to treat and even prevent some of the hereditary forms of heart failure. I also think that we are going to be able to identify some of the very early forms of heart failure with noninvasive methods and therefore start treatments for patients when they are not quite so sick, thus allowing us to make a major impact on the long-term morbidity and mortality of patients.

In terms of medical treatments, advances will come in several forms. We will continue to learn more about how heart failure develops from a very early asymptomatic stage to a stage of overt symptomatology. We will attack the disease in a multidimensional method using what Dr. Jay Cohn has called polypharmacy. I believe that in only a few short years we'll probably be using as standard therapy four and maybe five drugs to treat heart failure (and we can only wonder what impact that will have on the economic burden of treating our patients). I believe that there will be many advances in the field of transplantation, primarily coming with the development of a totally implantable artificial heart, which will avoid the current problems of donor shortage and requirements for immunosuppression. There will also be some advances made in the area of *xeno-transplantation*, that is, using animals to supply a heart for a needy human.

We will also see increased interest in nonpharmacologic methods of treating heart failure. There will be greater attention at all levels of medical care to some of the basics, such as fluid and salt restriction, and many programs will develop to encourage exercise training as a form of therapy for patients with heart failure.

It is estimated currently that one-third of Americans have used alternative medical sources within this country at some time within the past year. I trust that our knowledge and investigation of alternative methods for treating heart failure will accelerate to provide some scientific support and guidance for what could otherwise become mass mania among our needy population. It is frightening to see government cuts for research spending at a time when we need good clinical and basic research more than ever.

At a recent lecture I gave at a geriatric cardiology symposium I ended the lecture with two slides that said *The cure for heart failure in the elderly . . . is prevention of cardiovascular disease in the young.* In fact, the only cure we will ever have for heart failure lies in preventing the multiple forms of heart and lung disease that precede its development. We certainly are making advances in this country in terms of lowering the incidence of heart attack and stroke, but the problems still loom large. We must not forget that cardiovascular disease still kills more Americans than any other disease. We must totally rethink how we live and work in order to find ways to prevent cardiovascular disease, which attacks even our very young.

These are goals that will take decades to have an impact, but we must start now. We must convince industry and government that we care about our health and those of our loved ones. We must start now to wage a war on unhealthy behavior in general; only then will we have an impact on the health of this nation and finally have success with heart failure.

Appendix I

Glossary of Heart Failure Terms

Angina pectoris Literally means pain in the chest, a symptom that often occurs when the heart muscle does not get enough blood. This is most often due to clogged coronary arteries, the arteries that carry blood to the heart muscle. Sometimes, however, a person can have poor blood supply to the heart and even suffer a heart attack without having angina pectoris.

Angiogram A test in which contrast material or dye is injected into an artery to see if the artery is narrowed or diseased. A **coronary angiogram** examines the arteries of the heart.

Angiotensin-converting enzyme inhibitor (ACEI) A drug that blocks a key enzyme reaction in the body so that another potent enzyme, **angiotensin II,** is not produced. Angiotensin II causes constriction or narrowing of the arteries along with other detrimental changes.

Anticoagulation Inhibition of the coagulation or clotting process of the blood. Either weak hearts or hearts with certain irregular heartbeats, such as atrial fibrillation, are more likely to form blood clots, which can break off and spread to the lungs, brain, kidney, and so on. Medications such as aspirin or Coumadin are commonly used to "thin" the blood or prolong the clotting process so that blood clots do not form in the heart.

Arrhythmia   An irregularity of the heartbeat rhythm. Arrhythmia can originate in the upper chambers (atria) or the lower chambers (ventricles) of the heart.

Atrial fibrillation   A heartbeat disorder whereby the two upper heart chambers fail to contract or squeeze in rhythm with the rest of the heart; thus the heart loses the use of these two booster pumps.

Atrium (plural, atria)   One of the two upper chambers of the heart, designated as the right atrium and the left atrium. The atria serve both as reservoirs of blood and as auxiliary pumping chambers. Blood from the body (arms, legs, and so on) returns to the right atrium; when the right atrium contracts or squeezes, it pumps the blood into the right ventricle, which is the main pump on the right side of the heart. From there it is pumped up into the lungs, where oxygen gets put into the blood. After the blood passes through the lungs it goes to the left atrium, which then helps pump the blood into the left ventricle, or main pumping chamber on the left side of the heart, which sends the oxygen-containing blood back out to the body.

Beta-blocker   A medication that blocks or inhibits the effect of body hormones on the tissues of the body. A beta-blocker can slow the heartbeat, among other things.

Blood pressure   The pressure or force the blood makes in the arteries as it travels throughout the body. Blood pressure is a result of the contraction or squeeze of the heart plus the resistance maintained by the tiny muscles in all the arteries of the body. The **systolic blood pres-**

sure (top number) is the maximal force generated with the squeeze of the heart. The **diastolic blood pressure** (bottom number) is the pressure that remains in the arteries as the heart relaxes or "reloads" for the next heartbeat.

Cardiac output A measurement of how much blood the heart pumps to the body per minute, usually expressed in liters per minute.

Cardiomyopathy A general term meaning there is something wrong with the heart muscle. When there is a specific cause, another term may be added, for example, **ischemic cardiomyopathy,** where the lack of blood (see **ischemia**) or a heart attack has caused the heart muscle problem. Another example is **hypertensive cardio- myopathy,** where the cause is hypertension, or high blood pressure.

Catheterization Passage of a catheter or tube into an ar- tery or vein in order to make measurements. A **cardiac catheterization** records the pressures within the heart and lungs.

Congestive heart failure (CHF) See **heart failure.**

Coronary artery disease (CAD) CAD represents an en- tire spectrum of diseases due to blocked or clogged heart arteries, including **angina pectoris, heart attack (myocardial infarction**), or even **heart failure** due to poor blood supply to the heart muscle.

Cor pulmonale A special form of heart failure that in- volves only the right ventricle and is due to some prob- lem or scarring in the lungs. Many patients with emphy- sema, or severe scarring and destruction of lung tissue due to cigarette smoking (one of the most common causes), can develop cor pulmonale, which also pro- duces liver swelling, fluid in the abdomen, and leg swelling.

Diastole   The relaxing of the heart muscle as it "reloads" with more blood and prepares for the next heart contraction, or squeeze (see **systole**).

Digoxin   A medication that can regulate the heart rhythm and help the heart muscle beat stronger.

Dilated cardiomyopathy   A heart muscle problem in which the heart muscle becomes enlarged (dilated) and loses its elasticity (weakens).

Diuretic   A medication that acts on the kidney to help rid the body of more salt and water, thus increasing urination.

Dyspnea   The sensation that breathing is more difficult than normal.

Echocardiogram   A noninvasive test that bounces sound waves off a heart to determine its size, structure, and function.

Edema   Fluid, under excessive pressure, that leaks out of the blood vessels and gets into the tissue. Edema is commonly seen in the hands and legs and also in the tissue of the lower back. Your doctor can also "hear" the fluid when it leaks into the lung tissue; this is called **crackles** or **rales.**

Ejection fraction   The amount of blood the ventricles of the heart pump with each beat. For example, if the left ventricle holds 100 cubic centimeters of blood when it starts to pump and if it holds 40 cubic centimeters at the end of the beat, it has ejected 60 cubic centimeters. The formula to calculate the ejection fraction is as follows:

$$\frac{100 - 40}{100} \times 100\% = \frac{60}{100} \times 100\% = 60\%$$

Normal on the left side is about 50% to 60%, on the right side 45% to 50%. When your doctor says your ejection fraction is 30%, then, it is not one-third of normal but really one-half of normal.

Electrocardiogram   A simple test to check the electrical activity of the heart, including its rhythm, the presence of heart enlargement, or evidence of a prior or recent heart attack. An electrocardiogram is also called an **EKG** or **ECG.**

Endomyocardial biopsy   A sampling of the heart muscle that can be looked at under the microscope. The heart tissue is obtained by passing a special instrument into a vein toward the heart. This is routinely done after a heart transplant to detect rejection of the heart.

Etiology   The cause of a certain condition. A heart failure etiology would be the medical condition that caused the heart to malfunction, such as a heart attack.

Familial cardiomyopathy   A rare form of heart failure that affects several members of a family. This is an inherited form of heart failure, usually of the systolic type.

Gallop   Abnormal sounds that the heart makes in a variety of conditions, including heart failure or hypertension. These sounds are so named because they resemble the rhythmic sound of a galloping horse's hooves as they strike the ground.

Heart   A chambered blood pump made out of muscle. Its job is to pump the blood around the body and supply oxygen or fuel and nutrients to the body tissues and organs.

Heart failure   A problem that can be induced by many different causes; primarily means that the heart is not working as a pump as efficiently as it was meant to.

Heart rate   The number of times or cycles the heart pumps per minute. Normal may vary from about 50 beats per minute to 90 beats per minute at rest.

Hypertension   An abnormal elevation of the blood pressure (see **blood pressure**).

Hypertrophic cardiomyopathy   A heart muscle problem in which there is excessive growth or too much heart muscle. Usually, the problem is with abnormal relaxation of the muscle (see **diastole**).

Idiopathic cardiomyopathy   A form of heart failure in which no specific cause can be determined.

Inotropic   Medical term meaning to improve the contraction or squeeze of the heart muscle.

Invasive   A test or procedure that involves entering the body, artery, or vein. For example, a cardiac catheterization involves placing tubes into the veins or arteries. An invasive procedure usually carries some risk, albeit small.

Ischemia   Medical term for lack of proper blood and oxygen supply to any tissue. A heart attack is ischemia to the heart muscle.

MUGA (or Radionuclide angiogram [RNA])   A nuclear medicine test that helps determine the ejection fraction or pumping ability of the heart.

Myocardial infarction   The medical term for a heart attack. The usual cause is a blocked coronary artery, which prevents blood and oxygen from nourishing the heart muscle.

Myocarditis   An inflammation of the heart muscle. This can be caused by viruses or bacteria or may even result from an allergic reaction to medicines or drugs.

Myocardium   The medical name for the heart muscle.

Nocturia   Refers to getting up at night to urinate (see **paroxysmal nocturnal dyspnea**). Whenever the person with heart failure lies down, excess fluid may return to the heart; if the heart can sufficiently pump the blood down to the kidneys, urine is formed, which wakes up the person and signals him or her to go to the bathroom.

Noninvasive   Refers to a test or procedure that can be done without entering the body, such as an **electrocar-**

diogram or an **echocardiogram.** Usually involves minimal or no risk.

Norepinephrine One of the body's stress hormones that is secreted in increased amounts in response to stress or danger, but returns to normal when the stress or danger has passed. With heart failure, the body senses a constant stressful state and the level of norepinephrine goes up and stays up. This elevation can be measured by a blood test and is one of the strong indicators of prognosis in heart failure patients.

Orthopnea The sensation that breathing is difficult when you lie down.

Oxygen consumption (VO$_2$) A measurement of how much oxygen the body is using. With exercise, for example, the body's need for oxygen increases, and hence the oxygen consumption measurement goes up. The status of the lungs, heart, blood, blood vessels, and muscle all affect this measurement. When a person has heart failure, the total amount of oxygen consumption is low, in part because the heart can't pump the blood and oxygen sufficiently. The peak or maximal oxygen consumption can serve as an indicator of the degree of heart failure.

Paroxysmal nocturnal dyspnea (PND) **Dyspnea** is the sensation that breathing is more difficult, that one is short of breath. Paroxysmal nocturnal dyspnea, then, is the sensation of shortness of breath that comes on suddenly (paroxysm) at night (nocturnal). When people with heart failure accumulate extra fluid and are on their feet all day, the forces of gravity help push the extra fluid out into the tissues, thus forming **edema** (see **edema**). When the person finally lies down and the force of gravity is removed, the edema fluid eventually works its way back into the blood vessels and back to the heart. The weakened heart cannot sustain the extra fluid and some backs up into the lungs, causing congestion. The fluid in the lungs prevents sufficient oxygen from getting in through the lungs, and shortness of breath results. While this typically occurs at night, it can occur at any time—in the morning, for night workers, or even with a nap. Typically, PND occurs about 30 to 60 minutes after the patients lie down. They may wake up coughing, gasping, or simply feeling uncomfortable. They may then sit on the edge of the bed, go to the bathroom, tuck an extra pillow under their head, or go to sleep on the sofa or in a recliner. With the head elevated, PND may not occur.

Prognosis   A doctor's estimation, based on previous experience or medical studies, of what the outcome might be for an "average" patient with a particular disease. A prognosis may also involve an estimation of how long a person has to live.

Radionuclide angiogram (RNA)   See **MUGA.**

Sinus rhythm   The normal heart rhythm in which the upper heart chambers (**atria**) contract or squeeze in synchrony with the lower chambers (**ventricles**). Normally, the atria squeeze and help the blood pass to the ventricles; there is a wait for a fraction of a second while the ventricles fill completely, and then the ventricles squeeze. The exact coordination of the atria and ventricles is very important for maximal heart efficiency.

Swan-Ganz catheter   A **catheter,** or tube, named after its two inventors, that is passed through the right-sided heart chambers and to the lungs to measure pressures within the heart and lungs.

Systole   The contraction of the heart as it squeezes the blood out or the phase of contraction in the heart's two-phase cycle. The other phase, where the heart relaxes and "reloads" more blood and prepares for the next contraction, is called **diastole.**

Valve   The heart valves help direct the flow of blood in a single continuous direction. There are four heart valves: the two that control the flow of blood between the atria and ventricles on the right and left are called the **tricuspid** and **mitral valves,** respectively. The two valves that direct the flow of blood away from the heart are called the **pulmonic valve** (which directs blood from the right ventricle into the pulmonary artery and into the lungs) and the **aortic valve** (which directs blood from the left ventricle into the aorta, which is the major artery of the body and leads to all the other arteries). These valves open and close with each heart cycle (more than 100,000 times each day!). They are quite durable but can be damaged by rheumatic fever, infection, and even aging. When the valve becomes too narrow and not enough blood gets through it, it is said to be stenotic. "Regurgitation" occurs when the valve leaks and blood flows back through the valve in the wrong direction.

Vasodilator   A medication that dilates, or opens up, the arteries and veins of the body. This makes it easier for the heart to pump the blood since the heart meets less resistance.

Ventricles   The two main lower pumping chambers of the heart. The **right ventricle** has the job of pumping blood up to the lungs, where oxygen gets put into the blood. The **left ventricle** has the job of pumping blood to the whole body—the muscles of the arms and legs, the brain, the intestine, kidneys, and so on. Most heart failure results from some damage to the left ventricle, as would happen with a heart attack. However, the right ventricle alone can be weakened; most commonly, however, it is weakened when the left ventricle becomes weak and blood then backs up to the lungs and then to the right ventricle.

Appendix II

Resources for More Information and Help for Patients with Heart Failure

I would not have written this book if I thought there were sufficient sources of information for patients who suffer with heart failure and their families to turn to. I hope this book fills a gap, since that is its intended purpose. However, no book can be all inclusive, and I therefore want to list some of the other sources patients, families, and professionals can consult for more specific information as well as for information on related topics.

Professional Organizations

One of the best places to turn for more information is the American Heart Association. The national offices are in Dallas, Texas, but there are many local affiliates that can be found in most of the major cities within the United States. You should check your local phone book for the American Heart Association affiliate in your area, and a simple phone call will usually result in your receiving many free pamphlets full of information. The American Heart Association has a new toll-free service, and simply by calling 1-800-AHA-USA1 you will be connected with the local office in your area. Otherwise, you can always write to the American Heart Association at 7272 Greenville Avenue, Dallas, TX 75231.

The American Heart Association publishes a variety of pamphlets; these are usually quite up to date and expertly done. Most of them concern general topics related to heart disease, for example:

1. *How to Make Your Heart Last a Lifetime.* This pamphlet describes general ways to take care of your cardiovascular health, including exercise, weight reduction, checking for diabetes, cutting the cholesterol out of your diet, lowering your blood pressure, and quitting smoking.
2. *A Guide to Losing Weight.* This pamphlet offers some good tips and a very good section on calorie counts.
3. *Save Food Dollars and Help Your Heart.* This is a good guide to good daily nutrition, with a focus on a low-fat diet.
4. *Sex and Heart Disease.* While this pamphlet does not specifically address heart failure topics, it certainly is applicable to patients who have heart failure and is a good quick read on this sensitive topic.

One of the books I have used for many years is one published by the American Heart Association of Metropolitan Chicago. This self-instruction booklet is called *Congestive Heart Failure.* It was written back in 1985 and therefore is not absolutely up to date, but it has a very good introduction, some good diagrams of the heart, an explanation of what heart failure means, and excellent discussions of some of the common topics that need to be reviewed with heart failure patients. It also discusses a bit about medications and fluid and salt restriction. A similar booklet may be available from your local American Heart Association affiliate.

You may also call or write to the National Heart, Lung and Blood Institute in Bethesda, Maryland, to inquire about specific research areas in a variety of cardiovascular diseases.

Other organizations that may have some general information on heart disease and/or aging are the following:

American Geriatrics Society
770 Lexington Avenue
Suite 300
New York, NY 10021

American Association of Retired Persons (AARP)
601 E Street, NW
Washington, DC 20049

Council of Geriatric Cardiology
4101 Lake Boone Trail
Suite 201
Raleigh, NC 27607

Again, these organizations may not have anything specific on the topic of heart failure, but they do have some other general good references. The American Association of Retired Persons, for example, has a variety of materials available, including an excellent folder entitled *A Path for Caregivers*, which is a good resource for families who end up providing a lot of care in the home.

Don't forget to use your local hospitals as a potential source for information. Each of the hospitals I work at has developed informative literature that is distributed to patients and their families to take home. You may also want to talk to the hospital social worker, who can provide additional information regarding the availability of home nursing services and visiting nurses and who can frequently help arrange for Meals on Wheels, direct you to the local offices on aging, and serve as a liaison to some of the community-based services. For example, at one of our hospitals the social service workers frequently arrange free or low-cost transportation to and from subsequent office visits for all patients over the age of 65 who live within a certain community.

Support Groups

About 7 years ago I founded one of the very first support groups for heart failure, I believe, within the entire country. The meetings specifically addressed the problems, questions, and concerns of the heart failure patient. Often family members attended with the patient. We discussed many of the topics covered in this book, including fluid and salt restrictions, medication, and experimental trials. Unfortunately, that support group is no longer active, but others are springing up in various cities. While I cannot guarantee what the content, leadership, or goals are for each of these support groups, I recommend that if you find one in your area, you check it out to see if it is appropriate for you. Also, you might want to consider starting a support group yourself, perhaps with the help of the nursing or social service staff of your local hospital. I can tell you that the heart failure support group we ran combined an information session with a 15- to 30-minute talk—on topics ranging from salt restriction, to drugs, to experimental therapies, to communication skills—and a period of open communication. Almost all the patients felt relieved to know that others were in the same boat, and I think this is one of the major functions of any support group.

There are usually support groups affiliated with most heart transplant programs, but from my own experience I would have to say that heart transplant support groups are generally not appropriate for most patients who have heart failure. However, it depends on the leadership of such support groups.

The Mended Hearts groups have multiple affiliates based at hospitals throughout the country. These are groups of people who provide encouragement and support at monthly meetings to all patients who have some form of heart disease. Most commonly, the members are patients who have suffered a heart attack or have gone through bypass surgery, but almost certainly these groups include some patients with heart failure. In my experience, however, heart failure is not a topic commonly discussed at Mended Hearts meetings. You should check for the availability of such a group at your local hospital.

Because young people have other problems that aren't addressed in the Mended Hearts group, a wonderful organization called Young Hearts was founded several years ago by Julie Prochich. This organization, which started in Chicago, now has multiple chapters throughout the United States. I think it addresses the special concerns of the younger patient that aren't available in other support groups I have seen. If you are interested, you can contact this organization at: Young Hearts, P.O. Box 274, Brookfield, IL 60513.

Drug Information

As I mentioned in Chapter 8, there are various sources for drug information, ranging from your local druggist to on-line computer services. I want to emphasize the importance of talking to your local pharmacist using him or her as a resource. Also libraries and bookstores offer a variety of books that discuss drugs and usage in general. The *Physicians' Desk Reference* is an excellent resource, albeit quite technical. This book is published by the Medical Economics Data Production Company in Montvale, NJ 07645-1742.

Recommended Books

Many years ago I was evaluating for a heart transplant a woman who had a rather severe form of heart failure. I had been called in by her primary cardiologist just shortly after he had told her, "I think you need a heart transplant —nothing else can be done for you." Although she was scared and somewhat taken aback by the notion that she might need a heart transplant, the woman kept her balance and sense of humor, and in the end this fine, intelligent individual changed my perspective and approach to patients in general. She was one of the first patients who made me understand the emotions and thoughts involved in hearing the words *heart transplant* and *heart failure* for the first time. She wrote volumes of notes, which she shared with me, and I remember her words each day. I should tell you that she chose not to have a heart transplant, eventually entered one of our experimental drug protocols, and is doing exceedingly well today.

The main reason that I mention this patient at this

time is because she was one of the first patients to ask me for something to read about heart failure. There were, of course, the pamphlets and books that we give to most patients regarding fluid and salt restriction, but she wanted more. She wanted to know some of the technical details regarding the results of the clinical trials, which drugs might be best for her condition, and how doctors really go about figuring out what a person's prognosis may be. I will never forget the day she came for an office visit and ended up poring over my textbooks for about 4 hours. It was really at that point that I realized that patients should read some of the medical textbooks, as long as they know up front that everything in the book does not apply to them and as long as their doctor is available to interpret some of the information for them. Therefore, I am going to list here some medical textbooks that you may be able to find in your local library, a university medical library, or a hospital medical library. Perhaps your doctor will let you read his or her copy.

Heart Disease: A Textbook of Cardiovascular Medicine, edited by Dr. Eugene Braunwald and published by W. B. Saunders, Philadelphia, 1994. This is a general cardiology textbook, but it has a superb section on heart failure. This book has recently been updated, and I would suspect that after reading *Success with Heart Failure* most people could easily read through the appropriate chapters in this textbook and understand most of the information presented.

The Heart, edited by Dr. J. Willis Hurst and published by McGraw-Hill, New York, 1992. This is a standard general cardiology text with a very good section on heart failure, one that would be quite comprehensible to most readers of this book.

The Guide to Cardiology, edited by Dr. Robert A. Kloner and published by LeJacq Communications, New York, 1990. This is one of the more readable texts and has very good sections describing some of the common cardiac diseases and the tests that are done to diagnose them. This is available now in a soft cover and would be a good general heart book to flip through as well as a good resource to consult for information on heart failure.

Congestive Heart Failure: Pathophysiology, Diagnosis, and Comprehensive Approach to Management, edited by Drs. Jeffrey Hosenpud and Barry Greenberg and published by Springer-Verlag, New York, 1994. This is one of the first medical textbooks dedicated to the topic of heart failure. This excellent resource is extremely detailed and very current. It also has an exhaustive bibliography, so readers who are so inclined can find the original medical articles and go through them.

A Color Atlas of Heart Disease: Pathological, Clinical and Investigatory Aspects, written by Drs. George C. Sutton and Kim M. Fox and published by Current Medical Literature, London. This is a fascinating book that describes pathological features of the heart in case histories of patients with a variety of cardiac diseases as revealed through such techniques as the electrocardiogram, the chest X-ray, and the angiogram. I think this would be fascinating reading for most patients.

The Ciba Collection of Medical Illustrations, prepared by Frank H. Netter, M.D., edited by Frederick Yonkman, M.D., Ph.D., and published by Ciba-Geigy Corporation, West Caldwell, New Jersey, 1992. Most medical libraries have a copy of this collection, and Volume 5 is the one regarding the heart. These are superb illustrations, and I believe most readers would find these fascinating.

The Living Heart Brand Name Shoppers' Guide, written by Drs. Michael DeBakey and Antonio Gotto, Jr., along with Dr. Lynn Scott and John Foreyt, and published by Master Media, Ltd., New York, New York. There are a great many books on food and the heart, but I think this is the very best one. It has some general information about different food groups, but its strength is that it lists virtually every brand name of processed food, along with its calorie count, fat content, cholesterol content, and sodium content (so you need never exceed your 2-gram sodium restriction again).

You Can Live with Heart Failure: What You Can Do to Live a Better, More Comfortable Life, written by Dr. Robert DiBianco for the Bristol-Myers Squibb Company. This booklet has been available for several years and is one of the best overall guides I have seen regarding heart failure. Dr. DiBianco, who practices in the Washington, DC, area, is one of the country's outstanding cardiologists. The booklet, which contains some excellent points regarding heart failure, is distributed by the pharmaceutical company and may be available in your doctor's office.

A Resource Directory for Older People, published by the National Institute on Aging. This book, which elderly patients with heart failure will find helpful, is the National Institutes of Health publication number 93-738. You can obtain more information on the book from the National Institute on Aging, Public Information Office, 9000 Rockville Pike, Building 31, Room 5C27, Bethesda, MD 20892. The phone number is (301) 496-1752. The publication service toll-free number for the National Institutes of Health is (800) 222-2225.

Love, Medicine and Miracles, written by Dr. Bernie S. Siegel and published by Harper & Row, New York, and *How to Live Between Office Visits,* also written by Dr. Bernie S. Siegel and published by Harper Collins, New York. I cannot overemphasize how important maintaining good mental health is for your success with heart failure. To my mind, no one has done more to raise the consciousness of patients and physicians alike and to teach them to communicate and explore their feelings together than Dr. Bernie S. Siegel. He has written several books—these two are my favorites—that primarily focus on his experiences in helping cancer patients deal with their emotions, but his messages of love and hope teach all patients, regardless of their medical condition, how to love life and regain health. His books can be read by virtually everyone, and I recommend them highly.

Miscellaneous

You should be aware that the American Heart Association holds a national meeting every November. Over 25,000 physicians, scientists, and nurses attend this meeting. Major advances in treating heart disease are frequently announced at this meeting and are then reported in the news media. The American College of Cardiology has its annual meeting in March of each year, and this is another time when you are likely to hear about advances in heart failure care and treatment.

Finally, let me suggest the usefulness of signing up at your local hospital or community college to take an American Heart Association–sponsored cardiopulmonary resuscitation course (CPR) or one of the more advanced lifesaving courses. Not only will the skills you acquire help to allay the anxiety and sense of helplessness you may feel about the heart disease of a loved one, but you will feel a great deal of satisfaction in knowing that you possess knowledge and techniques that can be applied anywhere to save a life.

Appendix III

Photographs of Hearts

In my office I use several graphics to help explain to patients what heart failure is, what a heart attack is, where the left ventricle is, and so on. I suggest that you may well want to go to your library to get a general health book, medical book, or even *Gray's Anatomy* to review the basic structure of the heart.

I have included in this appendix several photographs of hearts demonstrating some form of heart failure. I would hope that you see in these photographs the beauty of the heart as well as a clear image of what the specific problem with each heart is. I specifically want to thank Dr. William C. Roberts, who was the chief of the Pathology Branch of the National Heart, Lung and Blood Institute, National Institutes of Health, Bethesda, Maryland, and who taught me so much about cardiac pathology and heart disease in general. It was in his laboratory that photographer Margaret Moore Bartlett captured on film the serious nature of heart disease.

The photographs on the following pages are accompanied by a brief description. You may want to consult the glossary as you study these photographs.

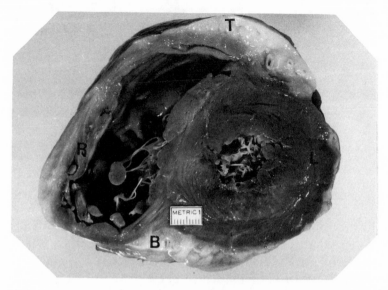

In this photograph we are looking up at a normal heart after a portion of the bottom two chambers has been sliced off. On the right side of the photograph is the left ventricle, with its thicker muscle, and on the left is the thinner right ventricle. Looking in the center of each ventricle, you can see portions of the heart valves, which direct the flow of blood in the heart. The one seen in the center of the left ventricle is the mitral valve, and the one in the right ventricle is the tricuspid valve. In all these photographs the part of the heart at the top of the photograph is the part that faces the front of the body, and the bottom faces the back. As a point of reference, it is believed that when a person dies, almost without exception, the heart becomes fixed in the squeezing phase, or systole.

Abbreviations: B = bottom or back portion of heart; L = left ventricle; R = right ventricle; T = top or front of heart.

Here the bottom pumping chambers of a normal heart, or the ventricles, have been removed and sliced into several layers. In each layer the thicker left ventricle is on your right, and the right ventricle is on your left. You may notice a small amount of lighter fat on the surface of the heart, and this is normal. In this heart there is no scarring, as from a heart attack; the chambers are not dilated, or enlarged; and they are not excessively thickened.

Abbreviations: L = left ventricle; R = right ventricle.

This photograph is a cross section of the ventricles giving an example of systolic heart failure due to ischemic cardiomyopathy, or heart failure due to lack of proper blood flow to the heart through the nourishing arteries of the heart. This patient had at least two heart attacks. You can see several white flecks in the back portion of the left ventricle (#1), which are areas of scar tissue from a heart attack. There are similar scars in the front portion of the left ventricle (#2), which represents another heart attack. This patient had heart failure for many years, beginning just after the second heart attack. Compare the enlarged left ventricle with that of the normal heart. This is the kind of heart that cannot squeeze well, and therefore there is poor pumping of blood to the rest of the body.

METRIC 1   2

This is another example of an ischemic cardiomyopathy due to coronary artery disease. You see here a large area of white scar tissue on the far side of the left ventricle, which is called the lateral wall of the heart. The scar tissue represents a large heart attack that occurred in the past. Notice how thin this portion of the left ventricle is in comparison to the neighboring areas. Following a heart attack, the involved portion of the heart muscle becomes thinner, and this thinning occurs quite early. Therefore, in the first few days after a heart attack, that is, before strong scar tissue forms, the heart can indeed develop a hole or tear in it, and this is called a rupture of the myocardium. Fortunately, the scar that develops during the healing process is quite strong, and further ruptures do not occur. After a heart attack in which one portion of the ventricle is damaged, the adjacent areas take over the work; in fact, the muscle in these areas can thicken, or hypertrophy, which is why the area near the large scar in this photograph looks thicker than normal.

Now look carefully at the top portion of the left ventricle (#1), and you will see a darker area of this muscle. This is a fairly recent heart attack. In fact, this patient had no symptoms of heart failure following the first heart attack, although it seems to have been a relatively large one. However, with the second heart attack the patient came into the hospital severely short of breath and in congestive heart failure and died shortly thereafter because of a serious irregularity of heartbeat.

This is a view of the heart cut in half from top to bottom, with the front separated from the back. We are looking inside at the back portion and have a view of all four heart chambers. The atria are on the top, and the ventricles are on the bottom. This patient suffered from dilated cardiomyopathy. There is no area of scar tissue or evidence of recent heart attack here, but notice that all four chambers are enlarged, which is typical in dilated cardiomyopathy. Although no cause for this patient's cardiomyopathy was ever found (and thus it is called idiopathic dilated cardiomyopathy), other cardiomyopathies, such as alcoholic or peripartum, could look identical to this. Note the delicate and beautiful valve structures. Abbreviations: LA = left atrium; LV = left ventricle; M = mitral valve; RA = right atrium; RV = right ventricle.

This is a transverse slice of the ventricles demonstrating heart failure is due to systemic hypertension, or high blood pressure. Notice how thick the left ventricle is. In response to the high blood pressure the heart faced with each beat, the muscle of the left ventricle thickened or hypertrophied in order to handle the load, much as the muscles of the arms or legs enlarge in response to a constant form of exercise.

Although you can't see them, there are also many small areas of scar tissue in this thick muscle. Compared to the normal heart, the actual cavity or space the blood would fill is much smaller. Because of the difficulty this kind of muscle has in relaxing, owing to its thickness, the small scars, and the relatively small chamber or cavity, it is harder for the blood to properly fill this chamber during the reloading period. As a result, not only does less blood get out to the body with each stroke or contraction but there is a tendency for blood to back up into the left atrium. This situation is a good example of what is called diastolic heart failure. As is typical in this disease, this patient, who died at age 68, also had kidney malfunction and a stroke, all due to the high blood pressure.

This is a photograph of a heart with a special form of diastolic heart failure known as hypertrophic cardiomyopathy. The heart has been sliced to show the left atrium and the left ventricle. The muscle of the left ventricle has grown excessively, especially the septum, or the portion that divides the right ventricle from the left. Notice how there really is only a very tiny cavity where the left ventricle normally is.

Patients can have multiple problems related to this disease, which can be hereditary, including heart failure with shortness of breath both at rest and with exercise, chest pains, and serious irregular heartbeats. In fact, this patient was a 23-year-old who died suddenly after climbing some stairs; other family members had the same disease.

In this photograph the left ventricle is actually quite normal in size and there is no evidence of a previous heart attack. Notice, however, that in this case the right ventricle (on your left) is quite dilated. This person had what is called cor pulmonale. This is a form of heart failure in which the right ventricle becomes weak and dilated owing to some problem in the lungs.

This patient was a 72-year-old with severe emphysema, or lung scarring due, in his particular case, to years of cigarette smoking. As a result of the lung damage, the pressure in the lungs rose, and each time the right ventricle pumped blood up to and through the lungs, it met a pressure that was more than 400% of normal. Eventually, the right ventricle failed to keep up this tremendous work, and right heart failure developed. The patient died with severe swelling of the liver, abdomen, and legs.

Appendix IV

Feedback for Doctor Silver

The process of writing this book accomplishes one of my lifelong goals. As I said in the very beginning, my single motivation for writing this book has been the tremendous need my patients have expressed over the years. I started with the idea of simply putting together a brief pamphlet that patients could take home to share with their families and that would answer some of the common questions regarding heart failure. That pamphlet has blossomed into what I hope will be a very useful but not burdensome book that will serve as a resource for patients, families, and health professionals.

On the other hand, I am 100% sure that I have not included every special situation or answered every single question that people may have about heart failure. And I am sure that my readers have had experiences in coping with their heart failure that many others could benefit from. I am not promising to ever write an update to or another edition of this book, but I would certainly welcome the opportunity to hear your comments about this book and to receive suggestions you may have from your own experiences dealing with heart failure. I promise at the very least to pass your ideas and suggestions on to my patients, and should the situation arise, I will certainly include them in an updated version of this book. Nothing would please me more than to be able to update the book in a few years' time to discuss the new cures for heart failure.

In the meantime, please feel free to write down whatever comments, thoughts, or suggestions you may have and send them directly to me at this address:

Marc Silver, M.D.
c/o Success with Heart Failure
P.O. Box 2124
LaGrange, IL 60525

Index